The Price of My Soul

The
PRICE of
MY SOUL

BERNADETTE
DEVLIN

VINTAGE BOOKS
A Division of Random House
New York

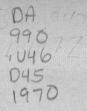

My warm thanks go to
MAUREEN McCONVILLE
of Observer Books and Features Ltd.
for help in preparing this book.

Foreword

The Price of My Soul is not a work of art, an autobiography, or a political manifesto. Readers who expect one or other of these things will no doubt class it as a failure. Let them. I'm not basically concerned with its success, financial or literary.

I have written this book in an attempt to explain how the complex of economic, social, and political problems of Northern Ireland threw up the phenomenon of Bernadette Devlin.

I also want to tell the story of the protest movement which wrote Northern Ireland across the world's headlines in 1968 and 1969. Because it is an account of my own impressions, it may not always be objectively accurate. If I have misinterpreted the civil-rights movement at any point, I apologize to my friends for it. In this movement, which is still struggling to free our people from the bonds of economic slavery, I am only one among hundreds of my generation. We were born into an unjust system; we are not prepared to grow old in it.

Finally, before I get submerged in all the Joans of Arc and Cassandras and the other fancy labels people stick on me, I want to put the real flesh-and-blood Bernadette Devlin on record.

The title has a family significance. My mother—whose life story was much more worthy of being recorded than mine—planned to write her autobiography under this title. Since she more than anyone was responsible for my attitude toward life and its misery, I have taken the title of her unwritten book. For this I apologize only to the members of my family.

The Price of My Soul refers not to the price for which I would be prepared to sell out, but rather to the price we all must pay in life to preserve our own integrity.

To gain that which is worth having, it may be necessary to lose everything else.

The Price of My Soul

Chapter 1

Socially my father was the bottom Cookstown could produce. He was the road sweeper's son. My grandfather had
served with the British Army in the Boer War, got a bullet
in his knee, and was rewarded with a job as a road sweeper.
He also got the tenancy of one of St. Jane's Cottages, a row
of cottages in Cookstown reserved for veteran soldiers, and
that was where my father and the rest of his large family
grew up.

My father, John James Devlin, was born in 1910 at Farna-
mullen, in County Fermanagh, but when he was two or
three years old, the family came back to Tyrone, their
county of origin. Cookstown, in North Tyrone, is a planter
town, one of several built in the seventeenth century for the
Scots Presbyterians who were imported into Ireland to keep
the natives in order. The structure of Cookstown hasn't
changed in the three hundred years of its existence. At one
end is the Old Town, the original settlement, which is
Protestant to this day. At the other, where the rebels once
camped, now stands the Catholic area. And the street which
in the seventeenth century joined the two ends, and where

merchants of both creeds met, still caters for commerce, whether Catholic or Protestant.

Cookstown is a Devlin area. For miles around everybody is called either Devlin or Quinn and they are all related to each other. This makes for problems in knowing whom you are talking about, and one way out of the difficulty is to call a man by his father's name as well as his own: John Pat Devlin, meaning John-Devlin-son-of-Pat. But the main way of differentiating between one Devlin and another is by the clan he belongs to, and there are dozens. My mother's name was Devlin even before she married. She came from the Ban Devlin clan, the "fair-haired Devlins." Another set was the Dubh, meaning "dark-eyed," Devlins. In recent generations, my father's clan was known as the "Fighting Devlins"—because that's all they ever did—but their earlier name was the "Delphy Devlins" or the "Hawker Devlins," because for years they had been travelers selling china and delft pottery and so forth. This was another bad mark for the family: not only were they working class, but they had a tinker background. The good respectable people in my mother's clan were very free with the "Hawker Devlin" insult.

Because of his family's poverty, my father left school when he was eleven and became a messenger boy, an unpaid messenger boy. Or at least, he was paid in kind: instead of a wage he earned some of the family's weekly groceries. But he was clever enough to see there was no future in this and when he was fourteen or so he apprenticed himself to a carpenter and got himself a trade. Over the years he worked on and off in Northern Ireland, but mostly he had to go to England to find work. To begin with this was merely because there was no work in the North of Ireland, but later—when I was already at school—he was forced to go to Eng-

4

land because his insurance card was stamped with the words "political suspect" and nobody in Northern Ireland would employ him.

He never found out why he was politically suspect. He had never been convicted of anything, but, though he tried from the bottom to the top of the civil service, he could not discover who had stamped his card in the first place, or why. His employer just produced his card one day with the "political suspect" allegation superimposed on it and told him he would have to leave the job. So thereafter he worked in England and came home to see us when he could.

I don't know whether my father ever belonged to a political party. If he had, he would have been a Republican. The Republican Party is another name for Sinn Fein ("Ourselves Alone") which was founded in the early years of this century to work for the political and economic freedom of the Irish people. It is the only political party that exists throughout Ireland, in both the six counties of the "British" North (where it is illegal) and in the twenty-six counties of the Free State South. Since the Treaty of 1921, which freed the South from British rule but severed the North from the rest of the country, the Republican target has been a reunited, socialist Ireland—an aim which for one reason or another puts the movement in conflict with the Establishment in both North and South. Part of the Establishment in the North, and deadly rival of the Republicans, is the Nationalist Party, the party of middle-class Catholics, who want an end to a separate Northern Ireland but are in favor of no further tinkering with the social system. The Republican movement has always consisted of two parts—the political side and the Irish Republican Army—and from time to time one of these wings has dominated the other. Ten years ago

5

the IRA was the stronger, campaigning explosively to "free the Six Counties" from English overlordship, and planning to work for socialism when the link with Britain had been cut. Today the political side has the upper hand and tries to preach a peaceful, political path to reunification *through* socialism.

Whether or not my father was a member of the Republican Party or of its armed wing, the IRA, his ideals were strongly Republican. He was the kind of man who would know lots of people in the movement and very likely he had helped some of them out when they were in difficulties. It was probably for some such reason that he was politically suspect. He got his Republican sympathies from his blind grandmother and, although his own father was once a British soldier, he himself had no love for England. He didn't hate the English, but he hated England and he hated the Northern Ireland system, both on historical and economic grounds. One thing of political significance that I remember from my childhood was my father wearing a lily in his buttonhole on Easter Mondays. We all knew what this meant: he was commemorating the Easter Rising of 1916. Officially it was illegal to commemorate the Rising, but being Irish the authorities tolerated what they had banned and lots of people wore Easter lilies. My mother, however, objected. Her attitude was that 1916 was over and done with, and Easter lilies were a pointless provocation to our Protestant neighbors; with our Easter Monday gesture, she said, we were just as bad as the Orangemen flaunting their banners in the name of past history on the twelfth of July. She was a very Christian woman. So every Easter Monday there was a disagreement: my father wore the lily, and my mother protested. But after his death she always put lilies on his grave on Easter Mondays—the significance being that this was the biggest argument they ever had.

My mother's background was entirely different from my father's. Both her parents came of good farming stock. According to family tradition, her father, John Ban Devlin, drove his horse and trap into Cookstown one day to look for a wife, met my grandmother's parents, and the marriage was arranged between them. My grandmother, Mary Jane McKeever, was twenty years younger than him, but it was a good farming match: he had the right breed of cows and she had the right number of pigs, and so on. So they were married, their land was amalgamated, and they came into town and started the pub that still exists. At that time it had stables and a forge attached to it, and with the business as well as the farm, John Ban Devlin and his wife were really well off.

John Ban Devlin didn't stay in the story long. He was a fine character but he had the family weakness of not knowing when he'd had enough to drink, so he sat in his pub, Devlin's, all day and drank the business into debt. He died when my mother was about two, leaving his wife four children and the debt-ridden pub that she could do with what she liked if she could redeem it. Subsequently, my grandmother remarried. Her second husband, Dan Heaney, had been in America and had amassed some small fortune there, and this was used to build up the pub, now named Heaney's, again.

The fortunes of the pub ruled my mother's early life. Because she spent most of her waking hours trying to work the pub into solvency, my grandmother hadn't time to be

7

a full-time mother, and when my mother was old enough to leave school it fell to her to run the home. My grandmother was said to be a beautiful woman when she was young, a very stately, straight person, with a sculptured, well-structured face and red hair. She was well liked and much respected in Cookstown, but to her own family she was a businesswoman: everyone had a moral duty to see that the work was done; there were no birthday parties for her children —parties were frivolous nonsense. Respectability and the business were the things that mattered.

My mother's name was Elizabeth Bernadette Devlin, but she was known all her life as Lizzie Devlin. She was born on June 13, 1920, the second daughter and fourth child of the family. She grew up to be the sort of stubborn, awkward child who doesn't behave like good, well-bred, main-street children should. She was always getting into trouble for not observing the rituals of Cookstown's bourgeoisie, which at that time had a lot of influence.

Her education came to an end when she was fourteen— as soon as it legally could—and she was forced, very much against her will, to leave school. Her eldest brother had been sent to secondary school, the plan being that he should either become a teacher or a priest. He decided he didn't want to do either: he wanted to go to university. But the university was, from a good Catholic viewpoint in those days, a den of iniquity, and my grandmother refused to sign the form permitting him to go. After that, although he was an extremely intelligent person, he just drifted from one thing to another and ended up joining and deserting the British Army in two days flat. Then he cleared off to Dublin, where he would be safe from the army authorities, and has been there ever since. The next child in the family, my mother's eldest sister, was sent to school and training college and became a teacher as my grandmother intended. But no such plan was made for my mother. My grandmother's attitude was: Why pay for somebody to look after the younger children when I've got a perfectly healthy, capable daughter? My mother had a good deal of fighting spirit then, which mellowed somewhat over the years, and she refused to leave school. She had won a scholarship that would take her to secondary school, and the entire staff of the primary school was on her side. They were on her side, that is, until my grandmother arrived on the scene, making good businesslike, Catholic, strong-pillar-of-the-Church noises, at which the religious section of the teachers' support fell away from my mother. She was told she was proud and arrogant, that it was her duty to go home and help her mother who had such a struggle, and so on. And she caved in.

In line with her middle-class status, she had been given various "accomplishments," among which were lessons on the piano and violin. For a while after she left school, her music lessons continued, but at some stage they were taken from her for being the nasty, ungrateful wretch she was. But she wasn't a nasty, ungrateful wretch—just a peculiarly human creature born into an inhuman circle. However, she *was* an obstacle to family harmony, regularly disgracing her relatives by making disloyal remarks about them in public.

When she was sixteen or so, the people who lived next door to the pub invited her to spend a holiday with them at Portrush, on the north coast. And in Portrush she fell for a Protestant. Sammy was then a laundryman in Coleraine: he was a Protestant, he was an Orangeman, he was later to

9

serve in the British Army. From a respectable Catholic view-point, he couldn't have been less suitable. (Next to my own father, I personally respected Sammy more than any man I've known, and would have been proud to be the child of such a marriage.) Before the romance had time to develop, however, my mother went home again to Cooks-town, and there began the saga of the fallen arches to which, in the end, I owe my existence. It was, in fact, only one fallen arch, and it started as a pain in my mother's foot.

Now at this time my mother resented her position in the family and she wasn't prepared to ask any of them for sympathy or advice about her foot. She wasn't a Cinderella: they didn't overwork her, but she was there to serve the others. When her elder sister came home on holiday from college, for instance, she brought a suitcase of dirty clothes for my mother to wash. My mother's position had degen-erated from being the second, but equal, daughter to being everybody's kitchen maid. So she kept quiet about her aching foot and, as the days passed, a limp developed. This didn't help. The family's reaction was that my mother was limping out of sheer awkwardness; if the pain was as bad as she was making out, she would have said something. After a couple of months of limping, she was horrified to discover that she couldn't put her heel back on the ground and decided, rather late in the day, that there were such things as doctors. The local doctor was called in, diagnosed a fallen arch, and said he would strap up the foot into its proper position and keep it that way until it grew normal again. The unbandaging and rebandaging sessions, when the foot relapsed from its proper shape into its deformed shape, were, it seems, extremely pain-ful, and one afternoon when she was sitting in the kitchen with the doctor working on her foot, it got more than my mother could bear. She said it was hurting. The doctor claimed it wasn't and went on to say that she was getting neurotic about it and if she wasn't careful she would go mad. Whereupon my mother lifted her good foot and landed the honorable practitioner at the other side of the room.

This was the end: she was now behaving like the working-class kids whom she had insisted on playing with as a child. All hell was loosed on her by her scandalized mother, but she didn't answer back. Although she was by now seventeen, she still had a kind of Victorian attitude to answering back her mother or arguing with her. Not until she was twenty-four and had been two years married did she say, "No, you listen for a change." But that day, anyway, she was saved by the doctor: it was his belief that things were getting too much for her and she should go away for a holiday. As soon as she heard this, my mother hobbled round to the friendly neighbors and suggested they should take her again to Portrush—and to Sammy.

This time, she stayed for several months, still limping, taking seaweed baths for her foot regularly but getting no better. Finally Sammy decided that the Cookstown doctor didn't know what he was talking about and it was time to see a specialist. He took her to Belfast and the specialist there, a Dr. Wright, told her he would have to operate. The months of neglect had not just misplaced the bone: they had worn it out of shape so that it would no longer fit its socket. However, he would break the bone, try to repair the damage and smooth the bone back into its socket as well as he could. At least she would be able to put her heel on the ground again, but she would probably have a limp for the rest of her life. At the prospect of surgery, my mother was up and out of the hospital and off: she would rather hobble than go through that procedure. But Sammy was firm: he dumped her back into the hospital, Dr. Wright operated and sent her home on crutches.

Back in Cookstown, life was just about as miserable as it could be. Here she was on crutches, perhaps for good, and the man she wanted to marry was a Protestant. She started going every day to church and she struck up a bargain with the Sacred Heart: if her limp went away, she would behave herself and renounce her Orangeman, Sammy. Sammy was a decent chap. He didn't believe in her Sacred Heart or her promises: the good God was an Orangeman, and he was well aware of the fact. But he said if that was the way she wanted it, fair enough, they would see whether the Orangeman or the Sacred Heart would win. The Sacred Heart won in the end. Dr. Wright had done a good job and her limp was getting slighter. Soon the crutches were exchanged for a walking stick, but my mother still hobbled to church at seven o'clock every evening to sit there and snivel and cry and feel sorry for herself.

Now at this time my father used also to spend an hour in church every evening, praying for help and guidance. He had two things on his mind: he was just finishing his job with the carpenter he had been apprenticed to and he was praying for some kind of outlet, because he didn't want to become, like so many people at that time, a skilled unemployed worker. And secondly, he was in a very similar situation to my mother, in that he had a lady friend in Belfast, Peggy Neely, who was not of Mother Church. Nobody in his family cared who she was, but *he* cared. He was at that time a much more religious Catholic than my mother, and he believed that if you prayed, things would turn out all right in the end, or at least you would be able to tolerate what you couldn't change. My mother was not at all religious in her youth. Religion to her then was the ritual of what was respectable, and she didn't like it and kicked against it. It wasn't until she was badly in need of a miracle for her foot that she discovered the benefits of going to church.

Anyway, here they both were in church, and, as my father used to tell the story, it was like the parable of the Pharisee and the Publican in the New Testament. Like the good, main-street Christian she was, my mother hobbled in on her walking stick, right to the front of the church, plopped herself down in the front seat, and began to cry and sob aloud, with absolutely no consideration for anybody else. The only other person in the church was my father, in the back seat like the Publican, kneeling very quietly and annoying nobody; and my mother never even noticed he was there. Finally he lost patience with her exhibitions and one evening he waited for her and said, "Look, I know it's none of my business, but do you think if you were to tell somebody what you have to cry about, you wouldn't cry about it so loudly? Then I could get on with my praying undisturbed." When my mother saw who it was standing arrogantly on the church steps as if he owned them, telling *her* not to annoy *him*, she was greatly angered. For all his low origins, my father had some prominence in the town. He was a very talented man, and he and some other young people were responsible for whatever social life Cookstown had. They organized dancing classes, they organized folk dances and concerts and hikes—ordinary, simple pastimes, but which wouldn't have happened without them. My father was a beautiful singer and he knew it. All round, he was, in my mother's view, an upstart.

But after that bad beginning, they got on better terms,

for at least they had a common problem to discuss. One day my father took my mother's walking stick away from her and disposed of it, and she found she could walk perfectly well. Through no miracle, but through human and psychological factors, her limp disappeared, and thereafter she walked perfectly naturally except when she was extremely annoyed or extremely tired.

So they decided to get married. Sammy and Peggy were not lost sight of: although they married other people in the end, they were always part of our family. As children we used to call Sammy "Uncle Sammy," and I must have been twelve before I reflected how odd it was that I had a Protestant Orangeman uncle.

My father set off for England to earn enough money to get married. It took him three years. He left Northern Ireland in 1939, when he was twenty-nine and my mother nineteen, but they did not marry until 1942. He, his brother, and another young man had work waiting for them in Coventry, but the night they arrived, August 25, 1939, there was an IRA attack in the city: a time bomb in the carrier of a bicycle left parked in a busy street exploded and killed several people. And because my father and the others were Irish, no one would give them lodgings. After wandering around for hours, they were given beds in a Salvation Army hostel, and from then until the end of her life, my mother was very kind to the Salvation Army.

While my father was earning and saving, at first in England and later, when he had refused to join the British forces, in the wartime Land Army in Northern Ireland, my mother was doing battle with her family. When they discovered that she planned to marry the road sweeper's son—a Fighting Devlin, a Hawker Devlin, just the bottom of the bottom of Cookstown—they set out to prevent it. They tried everything. They cajoled, they persuaded, they threatened, and they bribed. Since my grandmother's influence hadn't been effective, they called in the parish priest, Canon Hurson. He, of course, was supposed to take the part of the Establishment and put the weight of the Church's authority behind my grandmother's wishes, but being a priest of a rare caliber, he turned the tables on her. He took my mother by the hand and my grandmother by the hand, and said to my grandmother: "Mary Jane, yours was a made marriage. You know, and I know, that if you'd had your way, you wouldn't have married him. Be kinder to your daughter." And he produced a little homily for her about the true value of humanity and what really mattered in life. If, he said, she got another son-in-law half as good as the one my mother was planning to give her, she would be very lucky. (Years later, just a few months before my father died, my grandmother said to him: "Canon Hurson was never far wrong as a man, and he was definitely right about the kind of sons-in-law I would have." She was the sort of woman who couldn't say she was sorry, but this was her acknowledgment, after ten years, that my father was as good as anybody else.)

When even the Church failed her, my grandmother decided to use bribery to try to change my mother's mind; it was her last hope. Her first husband had left her the pub, burdened with debt as it was, to do with what she wished if she could redeem it. If she couldn't redeem it, it was to be dumped on the eldest son to see what he could make of it. But my grandmother *had* redeemed it, so she could now, if she wished, give it away. My mother was summoned, the family solicitor was summoned, my grandmother arrived and made her announcement: everything was to go to my mother—what was left of the farm, the house, the pub—everything would be hers when my grandmother died if she would wise up and leave the road sweeper's son. As she grew older my mother was surprisingly gentle-tempered, but in those days she was not. She just swept all the papers off the table and said they could keep the lot; she would rather have nothing. And the family resigned itself to the fact that nothing could be done to stop the marriage from taking place. But they still wanted no part in it, and as the wedding day came nearer, my mother and all her belongings were pitched out, bodily, into the street. She lifted up her cases, brought them all back in again, and said: "Right! Throw them out again! Every time you throw them out, I'm bringing them back in. I'm not leaving here until the day I marry, and I'm walking to my wedding out of my own house!" Well, they couldn't suffer the shame of it much longer: they couldn't keep throwing her out, it was attracting public attention.

The one thing that really hurt my mother in all this was my grandmother's refusal, even at the very last, to give her the traditional blessing. Hardly anybody turned up at the wedding. Naturally, given her views on the subject, my grandmother didn't go, and because she didn't, my father's parents also stayed away. Their attitude was: If our son isn't good enough for Mary Jane Heaney's daughter, then her daughter isn't good enough for our son. Altogether there were no more than six or seven people at the ceremony. So my just-married parents left all this family feuding behind them and set off for a honeymoon in Dublin, where they stayed with my mother's brother, Patrick, the brother who had scandalized the family by recruiting himself into the British Army one day and deserting it the next.

When they got back to Cookstown, they had nowhere to live. No one would take them in because no one was prepared to offend Mrs. Heaney by succoring her disobedient and ungrateful daughter. "We're very sorry," they said. "And, yes, it's terrible; but we can't *afford* to offend Mrs. Heaney." Once again Canon Hurson came to the rescue. Off he went to the town's exemplary Catholic, the leader of the Legion of Mary, the lady who went every morning to Mass and tore her neighbors apart on the way home, who charged exorbitant rents for poky little holes of lodgings, and he put it to her: "I know you're a good Christian woman. How about forking out one of your rooms for these two young people?" The town's exemplary Catholic was in a spot: Did you offend the Church or did you offend the merchants, when the merchants and the Church were in disagreement? She decided that you couldn't offend the Church, and begrudgingly she produced a room.

That was in 1942. In 1943 my eldest sister, Mary, was born. When my mother became pregnant, my father determined that he wasn't going to ask anybody in Cookstown to look after her. Cookstown had steered clear of him—not from personal animosity, but from fear of getting involved in Mrs. Heaney's quarrels—and he wasn't going to go crawling for any favors. On the other hand, he couldn't stop working and look after my mother himself: he couldn't afford not to work. He was working in Ireland then, on the emergency airstrip at Ardboe, and for months before the baby was due he worked all the hours God sent to make enough money to put my mother in a nursing home in Belfast. She stayed there for some time before the child was born, and for a couple of weeks after. And in Cookstown, where everybody's kids were born at home, this was regarded as the impertinence of the century—a carpenter, for Heaven's sake, with airs and graces! So Mary was born in a Belfast nursing home, far from the squabbles of Cookstown. Her sponsor, when she was baptized, was the midwife. The people my mother would have liked as godparents couldn't be invited because of Mrs. Heaney, and my father wasn't prepared to have anything to do with any of them. He was prepared to leave the child unbaptized till it was fit to pick its own godparents rather than impose someone from Cookstown on it.

A couple of weeks after Mary was born, my father went to Belfast to bring his wife and baby home. They got back to their lodgings to find all their possessions neatly ranged on the doorstep and, pinned on the door, a note saying in effect: "Children not welcome." Their so-exemplary landlady hadn't warned my father before he set off for Belfast; she didn't so much as tell him, "Don't come back." She waited till he had gone, then turfed out all their belongings and barred the door. So there they were, sitting on the doorstep like the Holy Family on its way into Egypt: one father, one mother, one child a couple of weeks old, and a town of Christians. They took a good look at their Christian town, and they didn't know what to do.

There was only one thing for it—my father had to swallow his pride and go to my mother's mother for help. But he only managed to half-swallow his pride. He asked my grandmother to take in his wife and child for one week and said that he himself would prefer to sleep in the street. At this point my mother introduced a complication: she wasn't going anywhere unless he went too, and before this ultimatum my grandmother gave in. My mother didn't deserve any favors, she said, and she knew the good Lord would punish her for her wickedness—in fact they were already seeing the punishment in operation. But she didn't dislike my father on his own account. Simply she could never accept his background. However, in the Christian charity of her heart, she would take in all three of them.

There they stayed, living with my grandmother, for about a year, and my mother's function in the household was precisely what it had been before she married: she did everybody's work for them. My father was tolerated. Although he lived in the house, he was never served a glass of beer in the kitchen as the other men in the house and even favored customers were. My father was an unfavored customer and he bought his beer at the bar. But he didn't care: his attitude was, since he paid for his beer, he could buy it where he liked, and at any rate Mary Jane Heaney served good Guinness.

Sometime before my second sister, Marie, was born in 1945, my parents got back their independence by renting two rooms above a milk bar in Molesworth Street. By no standards could you call it a desirable property. It was damp. It was falling apart. And it had rats. To get to the lavatory shared by all the lodgers, you had to pick your way through rotting boards on the landing, and my father spent all his spare time patching the place up. He put a gate at the top of the stairs to prevent us tumbling down into the street. The winter coat that my mother lost in that house has become part of the family mythology. She folded her coat away in the wardrobe one spring, and when she went to take it out next winter she found the rats had eaten all of it but the buttons. Or so she claimed, anyway, but we never quite knew whether to believe the story. However, rats or no rats, both my parents preferred living in independence and privacy to the comfort and servitude of my grandmother's house. At least the Molesworth Street rooms belonged to them. They paid the rent. My mother's favorite expression in life was: At least we can lock the door. As long as they could lock the door with everybody else on the outside of it, they didn't mind where they lived.

And then I was born. It was April 23, 1947, the feast of St. George, the patron saint of England, which I suppose has some sort of ironic meaning, though the anniversary I prefer to think my birth celebrated was April 23, 1916, the date of the Easter Rising. I managed to get myself born in the damp Molesworth Street house and promptly developed bronchial pneumonia and lumbar pneumonia and this and that and the other chest complaint. At six weeks old I almost decided I'd had enough of living, but survived that crisis to be shipped in and out of the hospital for some years to come. When the next child in the family was on the way, my father decided that we had outgrown the rooms above the milk bar, and off he went on his personal civil-rights action to the local council, demanding that they furnish him with a council house. We had been on the council-house waiting list all this time, but the local authority still wouldn't do anything for us. However, there was another possibility. The Northern Ireland Housing Trust, set up by the government at the end of the war to make some sort of impression on the country's chronic housing shortage, worked independently of local authorities in those days. So my father applied to them. To get a housing trust tenancy, you needed certain minimum qualifications: you had to prove you could pay the rent and would be a reasonably good tenant, and you had to have a reference. And here again we came up against the problem of the good charitable Christians of Cookstown.

Everybody knew there was no reason why my father shouldn't have a reference: he was hard-working, he could always pay his bills, he was never in debt. He was an ordinary, tidy, good-living creature, quite fit to live in a decent house with a bathroom. But nobody could be found to sign the reference. Everyone was afraid, all over again, that they would offend Mrs. Heaney if they assisted the renegades. One reason why I haven't grown up with the traditional Catholic idea of sticking to one's own is that at that time the only people who stuck to my parents in Cookstown were the good puritan Protestant Presbyterians. Two Protestant councilors signed the reference for my mother and father, and in August 1948 we moved into Rathbeg, the housing trust estate in Cookstown where we still live.

A whole house, all to ourselves—to begin with my mother didn't know what to do with all the space. But coming to Rathbeg solved the worst of our problems. My father went on working, sometimes in Northern Ireland, mostly in England, and the younger half of the family was born—Elizabeth in 1948, Patricia in 1950, and my only brother, John, in 1953. We had come up in the world. Where we lived the houses had whole floorboards and good doors and windows. If she had wanted, my mother could have got back some of the social acceptance that her scandalous marriage had cost her. But she wasn't interested. Lots of people who would never come to see her in the rooms in Molesworth Street now turned up to say how glad they were she had got a house; but they came when my father was out at work. My mother would say, "I'm very busy just now, but do come back this evening and have tea with us when John gets home." However, that was no part of their plan: they didn't like coming when John was at home. "Well, listen, my dear," my mother would say, "I don't want us to fall out, but if my home's not good enough for you when my husband's in it, you're not welcome in it when he's not." And that didn't gain her much sympathy.

Chapter 2

If it hadn't been for the fact that I had an essentially Christian background from my mother, poverty would have made me bitter rather than socialist, and what I knew of politics would have made me mad Republican. This is the common situation in Northern Ireland: if you don't have basic Christianity, rather than merely religion, all you get out of the experience of living is bitterness. My mother was, from my point of view, despairingly Christian. You could have kicked her fifty times a day and she would still have turned the other cheek—and not just in a passive way; if you had tripped in the action of kicking her, she would have lifted you up, knowing that as soon as you got on your own two feet, you were going to kick her again. Her life—the conflicts with her family, the loss of my father, the struggle to bring up six children on welfare benefits—gave two choices: she could either become bitter and reject everything, or she could accept that none of this really mattered because the world, after all, was only a stopping place. She chose the second. She had a kind of martyr complex, which to some extent has rubbed off on me. She had plenty of moral courage.

Her attitude was: if in your own conscience you know you are right, it doesn't matter how many people think you are wrong. Just plough on. Nobody will appreciate it, but you're not doing it for anybody's appreciation. You do it because it's right, and if it's right it's worth doing, and if it's worth doing, it's worth doing properly.

Her talk was full of these sayings from popular wisdom, such as "A thing worth doing is worth doing well." If you objected, "But I can't do it," she would say, "If there's a will, there's a way; the fact that you can't do it and give up means that you don't really want to do it hard enough." My father's philosophy of life was less reducible to proverbs, but I do remember two sayings he had. One was: "Your teeth are for keeping your tongue behind," and the other: "If you put your foot in dirt, it spreads. Just walk round it." And there was one observation my parents shared, and that was: "There'll be days when you're dead." When this phrase was used, it meant that we were going to do something rash, something we either couldn't afford to do or didn't have the time to do but that we were going to do anyway.

On this days-when-you're-dead principle, we used to spend two weeks at the seaside every summer—at Portrush, scene of my mother's early romance. When my father, being politically suspect, was obliged to work in England, we saw him only at Christmas and Easter and occasional weekends in between—he blamed and hated the English for that, and so did we all. But the big reunion of the year was the holiday at Portrush. As soon as Christmas was over and paid for, we started saving up. Tins of food to be taken on the holiday began to fill the top shelf of the larder. My father started cutting down on his weekends at home—these were expensive, not only because of the fares, but also because to make the journey worth while he had to travel on working days and so lose pay. As well as coming home fewer weekends, he would send home slightly less money, and save it up in England instead. My mother's one failing was that she couldn't save money: if she had spare cash and someone came to the door collecting for charity, or begging, she would give it away; if we had run up against our relatives and needed a morale booster, she would blow the housekeeping on something like strawberries and ice cream, and then we would be poverty-stricken for a week!

So my father did the saving, and when Portrush-time came around, we set off with enough supplies to last the family for a fortnight. Hardly any of the money went for food; most of it was spent on the rent of a house for two weeks, and on extravagances and pleasures. Not that we did anything very exciting. The older half of the family got up at seven o'clock to go to Mass with my mother and on the way back stopped at the harbor to buy fish and at the home bakery to buy bread; then they came home and we had breakfast. After this, all the swimming costumes, towels, and so forth were piled onto the push chair—there was always a push chair in use in our family, because there was always one of us of push-chair age—and we all set off together for the day, to spend the family savings on shows and cotton candy.

Because he died when I was young, my memories of my father are idealized. He didn't live long enough for me to start appreciating him critically, and I still have the impression that he knew an awful lot. It seems to me—and evidence from photographs bears me out here—that he was quite a handsome man. He was fairly tall, well-built, athletic: not at all the sort of person you would expect to die, as he did, of thrombosis. He had dark hair and a very firm jaw structure, which would have given him a stern face, but the effect was ruined by a large dimple in his chin—and by his eyes. Both my parents had the same sort of eyes, but my father's were more beautiful. They were pale blue, very calm, and honest, eyes that made it impossible for him to tell lies because they always gave him away. My mother, however, had eyes that made other people tell the truth: they were gray-blue and, like my own, rather round and staring. They were mystical eyes, looking through you rather than at you and dragging the truth out of you.

In her teens and twenties, my mother was a slight person. She must have had a large bone structure, but in those days she looked very thin and frail. Probably because she had six children she became in her thirties big and stout, and later she got very fat. She was in the end a great big moving bus of a woman. She was never healthy: her heart was weak and in her later years she suffered from angina and so she was obliged to walk slowly. She didn't look as if she was struggling along under the burdens of her weight and a weak heart, but rather as if she was walking serenely because life was much too good to be enjoyed at any quicker pace. When she got to the top of a hill, she would stop—simply because she *had* to stop to get the strength to walk on—but even then she looked as if she was pausing at the top of every urban hill to view the beauty of the surrounding smoke and chimneys.

In spite of working in England, my father played a part in the family that was unusual for an Irish father—or at least wasn't common in the circle we lived in. Other people's fathers' role was, it appeared, to earn the money, punish the children—"You wait till your father comes home!"—and let the wife get on with the housework. My father was a better cook than my mother and in fact taught her to cook all the things worth cooking, like fudge and toffee apples and pancakes. She had learned a mundane, square-meal kind of cookery when she lived with my grandmother, so when it came to Shrove Tuesday, it was my father who made the pancakes; at Halloween, he made the apple tarts and apple fritters and all sorts of sticky, gooey stuff for putting apples in. But he didn't just keep his talents for special occasions. If my mother had been pretty busy during the day, he would cook the supper—and we preferred it when he did, for he served us weird things that it was bad to send children to bed on. He thought nothing of doing the housework on a Saturday if he wasn't working, and was totally unashamed of hanging washing on the line—a thing most men in Cookstown wouldn't be seen dead doing. Cookstown in general thought he was round the bend: he had no masculine self-respect at all and was quite happy going shopping or pushing the baby's pram or buying clothes for his children. Other men waited for their wives outside the shop, looked uncomfortable, and carried the parcels. But Cookstown learned to admire my father because, although he was from the bottom, he walked with his head up.

My father was essentially a very gentle person. When he was working on the airstrip at Ardboe he noticed that the fellow beside him never brought any lunch, so my father used to bring double rations, share it out, and complain that his wife always gave him more than he wanted. After my father died, I remember this fellow coming to the house and telling us how gentle a man he had been. But along with

27

his gentleness, he had authority. At work he was always the one chosen by the men to talk to the management, and he was much more keen on discipline than my mother. He wasn't hard, but he believed very firmly that right and wrong existed: you should do the right thing for the right reasons, but until such time as you were prepared to accept the right reasons, you would have to do the right thing because you were told to. He had a fondness for the civilities of life, which was perhaps surprising in a working-class man. Since my mother came from the middle class, she could have been expected to insist on formalities, but instead she reacted against them. She didn't care whether or not we washed our hands before we came to the table, because she had been made to do it as a child, but my father cared very much, and he cared about how we treated the food we were given.

Once when I was seven or eight I came in late to tea, to discover that my sisters had eaten up all but one of the square ends of the slices of bread, which I—and they—preferred to the round ends. The one remaining square end was at the bottom of the plate, and I began flicking through the bread like the pages of a book in search of the piece I wanted. Whereupon my father slapped my hand from the table, looked at me, and said, "What have you done?" "Nothing," I said, big tears standing in my eyes. "Do you expect any other human being to eat the food you have rejected as not fit for your consumption?" "But Daddy," I said, horror dawning, "I can't eat five slices of bread—not with my tea as well." My father removed my meal, set down one empty plate, put the five slices of bread on it, and said, "You can have butter on them, you can have jam on them, you can have anything you like on them, but nobody is going to eat that bread but you. And if you can't eat it tonight, don't make yourself sick; it will be there for your breakfast tomorrow."

And I ate every one of those slices of bread. My father didn't put on this performance just to impress on me that one did what one was told: the important point was that I had not shown consideration for others, expecting them to eat what I had cast aside.

He was very strict about basic civil behavior. He was much stricter than my mother about people who raised their voices. Shouting, kicking, and biting were forms of combat not to be tolerated. We very seldom fought among ourselves, but neither of my parents minded if we did—so long as we fought it out and ended up as friends. But when a fight developed into a kicking and biting match, whoever was involved got the wooden spoon. The wooden spoon—an ordinary kitchen spoon—was my mother's punishment tool and the terror of our lives. It was kept in the knife drawer and once you heard the drawer open, you knew you were in danger. I don't ever remember my mother beating any one of us in a temper. She would sit there quite serenely, while things were getting out of hand, and say, "I'm warning you once—stop it! I'm warning you twice—stop it, or you will get the wooden spoon!" The third time, the knife drawer opened and the wooden spoon actually made its appearance, and my mother stood over the culprit: "Now, do you actually want me to use this, for this is your last warning." Usually we were smart enough to stop whatever we were doing at that point. If we were not, she very calmly led us away by the ear and spanked our backsides with the wooden spoon.

When we got slapped, it was always on the bottom, except for kicking, which merited a slap on the legs. But once I got a more unusual sort of punishment. In our kitchen we had a long couch, like a bench, which we sat along for meals in order of age: Mary, Marie, Bernadette, Elizabeth, Paddy, John—our place at table matched our place in the family. One day a fight developed on the bench, during which Paddy took a great bite out of Biff (the family's name for Elizabeth), unnoticed by anyone but me. Ever-valiant in the cause of justice, I came to Biff's defense and bit Paddy. And I was seen. Calmly my mother called me to her and said, "Roll up your sleeve." I looked at her, wondering where on earth the wooden spoon was going to fall, but I rolled up my sleeve. Still calmly, my mother lifted my arm and bit me as hard as she could—amid screams and roars and "No, Mummy, that hurts!" "Now that you know what it feels like," she said, "you'll not do it again in a hurry, will you?" It was against all the family traditions that I should say, "But Paddy bit Elizabeth first." Telling tales was forbidden: sisters should stand loyally by each other. If my mother caught someone doing wrong, she punished the malefactor, but if one of the others came in whining, "Mummy, do you know what she did . . . ?" it was the tale-teller who got the punishment: not only had she failed to prevent her sister from erring, but she had maliciously come telling tales as well. It was this curious discipline that made us all the peculiar characters we are.

Although, like me, my mother was careless of her own appearance, she made a point of dressing us well, and she dressed us all alike. Partly this was for economy. She was very handy with the sewing machine, and she used to buy material in vast quantities and make half a dozen dresses, identical in every respect except that each was a size smaller than the next one. So there we were growing up, and the frocks just moved along the line. But we were dressed alike for another reason as well: my mother had once seen this American Easter Parade photograph of an idiotic-looking family of about a dozen boys and a dozen girls—perhaps that's an exaggeration, but there was a massive row of children, and they were all dressed exactly alike. My mother fell for this photograph. I do believe at the back of her mind she cherished the idea that one day she might have five daughters and five sons, all dressed in uniform. It was a thought to horrify my poor father. "Just one boy will do me, honestly," he would say. "If we had that number of kids, we'd have nothing to put on them, never mind dress them all alike!" Occasionally my father would bring five frocks from England. The ones I remember best were blue and white with big, detachable white collars. Because they were prim and proper, they were English, and because of the collars, they were sailor; so we called them our "English sailor frocks" and we thought they were great. I can't think of another father who would have had the courage to go into a shop and buy five identical dresses, but it never cost my father a thought.

My parents' marriage was, I believe, more or less ideal: no one was boss; everything they did was worked out between the two of them, though I would say my father's word would have been final. There was a kind of mental telepathy between them that let each know what the other was doing and thinking and feeling, even when one was in England and the other at home. My mother used to ride a bicycle in those days and she was always falling off it. Once she had a worse fall than usual and that night when she telephoned my father—she used to ring him up about every other evening, just for three minutes—he said as soon as he lifted the phone, "I've *told* you to stay off that bicycle!"

Our family was a very democratic assembly: we were not a family in which there was a father who did a job, a mother who did a job, and the kids who did what they were told. As each one of us came to the use of reason, as it were, we were included in the family decisions. Once we knew how to count, we were involved in the family expenditure. We never had regular pocket money as children, but if we needed money for something, we got it. As long as the money was there, we could have it, even for frivolous and unnecessary purchases. But we were brought up to reflect that since we could get what we asked for, we ought to be pretty responsible about asking. If you wanted something only because someone else had it, you were forced to think, "Well, that's not much of a reason; I don't really need it," and reconcile yourself to doing without it. After my father died, this training paid dividends. We all took sick that winter—and this was another area where family solidarity showed itself: we all fell sick together. Once any sort of germ got into the house, we all came down with it at two-weekly intervals. And the only two people left on their feet on this occasion were Elizabeth and myself. Paddy, fretting for her father, had developed pneumonia; everybody else had the measles; Asian flu was hovering about; and the budgerigar died. And this house of mourning and sickness was run by seven-year-old Elizabeth and myself, aged nine. I couldn't cook—still can't—but she could, so I did the shopping, peeled the potatoes and did the humble unskilled work, and she cooked the dinner. "Well, she's got a good family," neighbors said of my mother, but they didn't interfere. We had lived independently of the entire town—not in isolation, exactly, but in a sort of unforthcoming friendliness. Now, instead of staying away from us because they didn't wish to offend the Establishment, people stayed away and hesitated to offer their assistance because they were afraid they might offend us.

We were brought up to ignore Cookstown, on the principle that it didn't care about us and we didn't care about it. Of course there was contact with our relatives. Sunday was walking and visiting day, and after Sunday dinner we used to set off in one direction to visit our wealthy grandmother, Mrs. Heaney; then five or six miles in another direction to visit our poor grandmother; and finally back home for tea. (My father used to turn these walks into educational sessions, teaching us about the rhythm of the farming year and to identify birds and trees. We weren't aware we were learning "natural history": it was just part of Sunday afternoons.) My rich grandmother helped us financially all our lives, but in a stern moral fashion that made it difficult to be grateful. She would send us a box of groceries and make sure we knew how much hard-earned money it represented, or she would give my mother money to buy us shoes, with the comment, "Don't say I didn't warn you!" But the contact with relatives didn't extend to their visiting us. Very few people came to our house, and I particularly remember one fellow who came for the first time after my father's death. He looked round at the books and the piano and the general air of comfort and civilized activity, and said, "My God, you wouldn't think this was a working man's home!" Remarks like that made me a socialist.

Because we were more or less related to half of Cookstown, we had simply dozens of cousins, and they all hated us. It could be pretty nasty in school. When they were feeling particularly spiteful, they would roar insults across the street at us, but on the whole we didn't carry our wounded spirits home. For one thing, we weren't really bothered, and, for another, we didn't want to upset my mother more than necessary. Mary, my eldest sister, and I—the two most precocious members of the family—would select and edit the version of the day's happenings to be told to my mother. However, if some stupid busybody of an adult had overheard the exchange of insults and could be expected to pass it on at home, then we had to tell.

There is no doubt that I owe the dawn of political feeling to my father. One way in which he was more involved in family life than most Irish fathers was in telling us bedtime stories. When I was quite little and he was working in Northern Ireland, and later, on his brief visits from England, he would put us to bed while my mother washed up the supper dishes. The stories he told us then were not about fairies and pixies, but the whole parade of Irish history from its beginnings with the Firbolgs and the Tuatha de Danain, the supposedly magical people of Irish mythology. He told us bedtime stories from recorded history as well—the battles and invasions, the English oppression and the risings, the English-Irish trade agreement that crippled the country's economy. Naturally he didn't attempt to be objective about all this: this was Ireland's story, told by an Irishman, with an Irishman's feelings. It wasn't until I went to grammar school that it occurred to me there were people who believed the Act of Union, making Ireland part of England in 1801, had not been brought about by perjury. To me it was accepted fact that Pitt and Castlereagh had conspired together and by every treacherous means under the sun had fooled everybody into signing the Act of Union. For that matter, I was surprised when I went to school that you had to learn about the Battle of Vinegar Hill or the decline of the Irish linen industry in formal history lessons. I hadn't realized this was history: it was something I had always known, from hearing it over and over again as a bedtime story.

Perhaps children do begin to develop a social consciousness from listening to stories about bad children being tortured by bad fairies and good children getting birthday cakes. In our family we developed an unconscious political consciousness from listening to the story of our country. The first nursery rhyme I remember learning was:

> *Where is the flag of England?*
> *Where is she to be found?*
> *Wherever there's blood and plunder*
> *They're under the British ground.*

My father taught me that jingle, and I used to say it as another child would say "Jack and Jill went up the hill," not relating it to England or feeling frustration or bitterness, but all the same acquiring a partisan outlook. "Don't say things like that," my mother used to protest, but my father would intervene: "Ah, it's good for them," he would say. And it *was* good for us. The songs we practiced to sing at children's concerts were never the "I had a bonnet tied with blue" variety, but "All around my hat I'll wear the tricolored ribbon." When I was about seven I could sing "The Croppie Boy" right through, and it has something like fifteen verses, each containing ten lines. At that age I suffered badly from asthma, and it was a battle of will power and a challenge to my physical failings just to get through fifteen verses, for

I had to stop to draw breath halfway through each line. "The Croppie Boy" is about a young lad who goes to the priest's house for confession, but after he has made his confession the "priest" jumps up, announces that he is a Yeoman Guard in disguise and that he holds the house for his lord, the king. The priest has been beheaded and is floating down the river. The Guard then kills the young boy. I don't remember singing this song with any feeling of bitterness: I was taught it for its beauty and because it was part of Irish culture, and it came naturally to me.

But such political lessons as I learned as a child came in indirect ways, through poetry and history, until I went at the age of ten to a madly Republican grammar school. If my father had any real involvement in politics, I never knew about it, but one circumstance suggests that maybe he had. He died in August 1956, just at the beginning of what the Unionists called "the IRA terrorist campaign," which lasted five or six years, with sporadic outbursts of violence and attempts at sabotage and so forth. At that time it was quite common to hear the sirens beginning to wail at night, up and down, up and down, as it must have been for air-raid alerts during the war. As soon as the sirens started, doors in our neighborhood would open and our neighbors would appear, pulling on their heavy coats and shouldering their Sten guns. Most of the Protestant men in our district were B men, or Specials—members of the civilian militia in Northern Ireland that was formed to fight the IRA. So while some of my friends' daddies were disappearing into their houses to lie low, other people's daddies were setting out armed after them. At times like those, the tragic division in Northern Ireland split even wider to set the Protestant working class against the Catholic working class, while the Church and the

Catholic middle-class Nationalists threw up their hands in horror at the freedom fighters, and stood solidly behind the government. The B men were pretty busy in those days: not in Cookstown itself, but beyond it on the way toward South Derry, where the land is poorer and the people, naturally enough, more Republican.

Just outside Cookstown, and lying between it and Omagh, there is an expanse of useless bog land known as the Black Bog. Invariably the IRA seemed to head for it, and none of them was ever caught there. Yet there was no cover: the Black Bog is like heath. If a man were to run across it, he could easily be seen. Perhaps they had a dugout in it, or perhaps they lay flat in the bog for a whole day; but for whatever reason, though the authorities put searchlights on it by night and sent helicopters over it by day, the Black Bog never gave up an IRA man. From our front bedroom window you could see, between two houses opposite, the beam of the searchlights traveling over the bog, and my mother used to stand there on alarm nights, looking across at the bog, and she would say, "At least they'll never get your father now." And even if we didn't know quite what she meant, we could guess.

Chapter 3

I remember the death of my father very clearly. It was a
Monday early in August 1956 and we had just come back
from our annual two weeks' holiday in Portrush. My father
had taken the seven-o'clock boat from Belfast on Sunday
evening to go back to work in England, and my mother,
that Monday morning, was feeling a bit down in the dumps
about it. To take her mind off her troubles, the woman next
door who had a sister visiting from Wales suggested that
my mother should go along with them to a linen sale. Earlier
in the year, to Cookstown's surprise, a linen factory had
managed to get itself burned down in the middle of a rainy
weekend, and as a consequence the stock was being sold off.
Bargain-hunting wasn't at all the kind of activity my mother
enjoyed, but she agreed to go anyway, and left us, cleaned
up and running around in the garden, with warnings that if
we played indoors we should leave the house tidy, and if
we got hungry, there was bread and butter and jam within
reach—she didn't want us to go climbing up the shelves.
While we were playing in the garden, Father McCrory, the
curate from our parish, drove up to the house and he and

my Uncle Barney got out of the car. We ran off to tell my mother, who hadn't set out yet but was still talking to her next-door neighbor, that she had visitors. Now my mother had a sort of fatalistic attitude toward life which was rarely proved wrong. As she came up to the visitors, she had already guessed that something was wrong and supposed it concerned my grandmother who was, by now, getting on. "Is it Mum?" she asked, and being a crafty, morbid child, I knew she really meant, "Is Mum dead?" Father McCrory just looked at her and said, "No. Come into the house."

I knew my father was dead. I had understood my mother's question, and from the way Father McCrory had answered it and looked at her, I knew that the truth was more terrible: my father was dead.

Mary, the eldest of the family, was the only one of us children not outside. She was upstairs reading. I sneaked upstairs, called Mary outside, told her what had happened, and suggested we should summon a conference, there in the garden, and prepare the others to be called into the house to hear the news. I was nine and Mary was thirteen. Being older and more sensible than me, Mary wouldn't let me tell the others. "If it's not true, it's an awful thing to say," she said. But neither of us thought of crying. My mother called us in then and I remember Father McCrory saying, "Do you want me to tell them?" My mother didn't need help, however. She took us all up to her bedroom, in which there was scarcely anything but the great big bed and a picture of the Sacred Heart, and sat us all down.

"I've got some bad news which is good news," she said. And Mary and I knew we were right. We just sat there, looking at her. Then John, who was three, began to cry because everything was so heavy and solemn.

"There's no need for crying," said my mother. "Nobody's allowed to cry. Your daddy's gone to Heaven, he isn't really dead."

At that Elizabeth and Paddy, who were the best criers in the family, broke down. Paddy could have been Cookstown's chief mourner, she could cry for anybody. You just had to take her into a church where there was a funeral and you would hear her sobbing like an old-time keener, embarrassing the chief mourners because she was doing a better job than they were. But now she had something to cry about; she cried all that day, and she didn't stop crying for about three months—but only when she was at home. Our attitude toward Cookstown prevented her from crying in public.

That Monday, after we heard that our father was dead, we dressed in our lemon-colored frocks with white collars and went down to my grandmother's, and on the way Mary and I broke a family routine. Usually when we went out together, we walked in line: Mary, Marie, Bernadette, Elizabeth, Patricia, with John walking at the back with my father and mother. We would sail down the street like a fleet, and if any of us fell out of formation, a reprimand came from behind—"This isn't Brown's cows!"—and brought us sharply into line again. "Brown's cows," it was understood, ambled all over the road. But that day we broke the formation. Marie walked between Paddy and Biff, and Mary and I walked in front, discussing the situation like two old grannies. Here we were at nine and thirteen: we had just been told our father was dead; the fact had been absorbed and put in the little computers; and we were busily working out what the reaction of our grandmother and our aunts and uncles would be. We were preparing for an unfriendly attitude on the lines of "It's no more than you deserve." But we also thought it possible that after despising him all his life, they would say, "Oh, you poor children! Your father was a great man!" So we were bracing ourselves to observe that it was a pity they couldn't have told him what a great man he was when he was alive.

When we got to the pub, everyone was in tears—everyone, that is, except my mother, who was the only person who was reacting rationally. We, the children, were ushered upstairs, and left to our own devices. Now, when we were on holidays, my father had taught us to play cards. We knew how to play poker, rummy, and whist. So while the adults were sobbing down below, Mary went down, got some money from my mother, and sneaked out to buy a pack of cards, and all afternoon we sat around upstairs playing poker. When the chief mourners came up to deliver the regulation tearful kisses, they were horrified. Back they went to report the scandal to my grandmother, and she came rheumatically up the stairs to try to persuade us to play something more respectable. But my mother wouldn't let her interfere: "Let them play poker," she said, and so we were left for the rest of the day.

My father died in England at the age of forty-six. He had left the boat at Heysham, in Lancashire, and taken a train for Dunstable. The train had gone through Morecambe and shunted back into the station to transfer to the main line. During this maneuver my father was taken ill with a heart attack, and in Morecambe station he was noticed by a porter. The porter wasn't a Catholic, but he had seen lots of Irishmen go through Morecambe and he suspected that my father was a Catholic because of the Pioneer pin he wore in his jacket, the badge of the Catholic total-abstinence association. My father hadn't always been a total abstainer, but one night he got very merry and suffered a bad hangover next morning, which decided him to give up drink. When he hadn't touched drink for a long time, he thought he might as well join the Pioneer Association and so get the spiritual benefits of belonging to it. And as a result he wore a little shield-shaped badge in his lapel, and it was this which the porter noticed. The porter carried him off the train, called an ambulance and, on the assumption that my father was Catholic, telephoned the local priest to say that an Irishman who looked as if he were dying was on his way to the hospital. The priest reached the hospital just as the ambulance arrived there, and he gave my father the last rites of the Church. Fifteen minutes later my father was dead.

During that fifteen minutes a nurse who was also Irish and Catholic asked my father if he wanted her to take any message to his family. He said he had no message to send, he wanted only to talk to the priest. People said he was a hard man to put the interests of his own soul before his wife and children, but my mother thought he had his priorities right. And I agree. What message, after all, is there to send when you have five minutes to live?

The remains were flown over to Belfast and my mother went herself to Nutts Corner, which was the airport at the time, to bring the body home. She always stated that my father's funeral took place in the early hours of that morning because it was only his real friends who went to the airport with her and sat up all night. The church was left open throughout the night, so that my mother, arriving very late from Belfast, could take my father's remains straight there, and avoid having insincere mourners coming to the house merely because it was the respectable thing to do. People who wanted to pay their tribute to my father could come to church. There must have been about six hundred people in the church: from Cookstown, from England, from Portrush—people like Uncle Sammy, who really cared about my father and mother. My mother almost made a witch of herself that night by leading the prayers in church after the priest had gone. To begin with, it was unheard of that anybody but a priest should lead the prayers in a Catholic church, and to have a woman do so only made it worse.

The next day was the funeral, the funeral of the husband of Mrs. Heaney's daughter. And because it was the funeral of the husband of Mrs. Heaney's daughter, my mother would not let any of us children go. Mary and I had been allowed to stay up the night before until the body was brought from the airport, but we could not go to the burial. We both felt it very much: we must have been morbid children. I really wanted to see the coffin put in the ground and the earth put over it, but they wouldn't let me go.

After that, two scenes stand out in my memory.

There is a big gateway beside the pub, which leads into a yard at the back of the building. I was standing at this gateway in a group with my mother and sisters and some of my uncles and aunts. Taking my mother by the hand, Uncle Tom said, "You don't have to worry about anything, Lizzie. We'll look after you."

"Huh!" replied my thirteen-year-old sister, Mary.

The second scene was in our own house, where we were all sitting together with the door closed. It may have been that same evening, or it may have been shortly afterwards. I remember my mother saying, "There are only the six of you, and me. We can depend on nobody else, so we must never let each other down."

And from then on we weren't a family, we were a cooperative society. Every Sunday morning we went to first Mass at half past eight in the morning, came home and made breakfast, then sat among the litter of the breakfast table all morning, discussing the past week and the week to come. At twelve fifteen, when it was time to hurry up and prepare the lunch, we would still be sitting there post-morteming on who had failed in their duties and why the place was in a mess. Before my father died, the house was regularly in a mess because my parents were tolerant about it as long as we tidied up when we finished playing. We could take all the cushions off the chairs and use them for horses if, once the fun was over, we put them back again. Now we began to notice that things got in a mess and stayed in a mess, because my mother was really no longer interested in tidying it up or obliging us to. So Mary decided that action had to be taken: she doled out jobs all round on the principle that since it was we who made the house untidy, it was our responsibility to tidy it up again. Sunday was the day for the job share-out. It was "It's *your* week on the stairs, and *yours* on the sitting room, and *yours* on making the beds." And it was the day for recriminations: "The stairs were only cleaned down twice last week; you'd better pull up your socks."

We did the shopping on Saturdays, so we knew on Saturday mornings how much money there was, and bought the groceries accordingly. Then on Sundays we would go through the accounts: "We only bought a dozen eggs yesterday, because there wasn't enough money for a dozen and a half. We'll have to go through last week's expenses and see what can be cut down on." Virtuously we would decide to cut down on biscuits: for a whole week we would buy no biscuits at all. But our budgeting always failed in the end, because none of us was any better than my mother about saving money. When it came round to Saturday night, if we had some money over, we went out and bought ice cream. So we never got any richer.

After my father's death, my mother became totally unworldly, almost insanely unworldly. She lived because she had six children who needed her. She lived for them. Life for herself held nothing. It must have been two years after my father's death before my mother bought a newspaper. She got up in the morning, and got us up; we all went about our separate business; and at eight o'clock in the evening, when we went to bed, she went to bed too. Sometimes she sat up later, just thinking, or reading, or praying, and on those nights Mary or I would get out of bed again and join her. She never looked on my father as dead in the sense of no longer existing. Because she was a very strong, convinced Christian, she considered he was not dead in the spiritual sense and she could still draw strength from his existence, as it were. She needed strength, because it was quite a struggle bringing us all up without a husband. We lived mostly on welfare benefits—her widowed mother's allowance, family allowance, and supplementary benefits. I used to get very incensed at the attitude of the civil servants whom we had to see about welfare. We were entitled to the money. My father had worked and paid insurance all his life, but they made us feel they were paying out money to the unworthy poor who had the bloody cheek to be orphans. I'm not a socialist because of any high-flown intellectual theorizing: life has made me one.

Our poverty wasn't extreme, but it was a kind of bottom-level poverty, the minimum necessary to support life in decency. It was of the order that my mother could say at tea-time, "If you eat up all the bread, there won't be anything for breakfast tomorrow." We got help, both in money and in kind, from my mother's relatives, which was more or less grudgingly given according to their more or less generous characters. Uncle Barney was by far the most kind-hearted of them all—and he was ashamed of it: he wanted to be a businessman, but he couldn't achieve it. He had no head for money and just threw it around him. He would very willingly give us money for nothing. One of us would call in to see him when we were downtown, and he'd throw us ten shillings, saying, "Buy yourselves some sweets." But he always wanted to *see* what we had bought, so he could be sure that it was properly frivolous. Every time he saw us, he'd ask, "Did you buy those sweets?" and we'd have to put him off: "No, Barney, we're just buying them now." Then a brilliant excuse would occur: "Actually, Barney, it might be better if we bought apples." The point of this was that the fruit shop was on the way home, and Uncle Barney couldn't check up on our purchases, whereas the sweet shop was just next door. So off we went with our ten shillings, didn't buy any apples, and brought the money home.

Another time he might ask: "What are you eating for the tea out there?"

"I don't know, Barney."

"Are you not down to buy something for the tea?"

"No, we're not, Barney. We came down to the post office."

"And you don't know what's in the house for the tea?"

"We don't know, Barney."

None of us was ever going to say what we had at home to eat, because we would either get the reaction, "Have you nothing better than that?" or conversely, "You're wasting your money: bread and butter's good enough for you." You couldn't please them, so we adopted the attitude that it was none of their business what we ate for tea. But if at the end of such a dialogue, Barney gave us some money and said, "Well, go and buy some ham for the tea," we would buy something more economical than ham to feed the family with—tomatoes, or something—and bring the change home. He used to send us out fish on Fridays. They were all lords and ladies bountiful in their own way, but Barney was the only one who gave because he liked doing it; only now and again he got ashamed of this generous streak.

What maddened me most was having money *thrown* at me, and once I threw it back. It was the Christmas before my mother died, Christmas 1966. One of my uncles threw me £5 in pound notes, saying, "Don't squander that; it's for Christmas." He meant to land it on the table, but it slid right across and fell on the floor. I picked it up, threw it on the floor at his feet, said, "It won't be squandered if you spend it," and walked out. While I was walking home, he was round in the car before me, slamming this crumpled £5 down on the table and telling my mother that I might at least be grateful, for he was trying to help. My mother refused it; he wouldn't take it back; so she just literally threw the money in the fire, and they both sat there watching pound notes burning.

There were other people who helped us as well as our relatives. A wee Protestant woman who lived across the road was one of the most genuine friends we ever had, and one of the most discreet givers. If she noticed we were short of something, she would just leave it for us without any fuss. At Christmas she would bake us cakes, and so on. You could say she helped to bring me up. She was a deeply religious woman who thought the world of my mother and respected my mother's religious beliefs, for all that they were different from hers. She even came to the Catholic church for my mother's funeral. But when, in April 1969, I was fighting the Mid-Ulster by-election campaign, she stood in the streets of Cookstown and howled at me, "You Fenian scum!" All because of the Reverend Ian Paisley, and civil rights, and unemployment. Since then she has not spoken to me, but slams the door when she sees me coming.

Chapter 4

Should an anthropologist or a sociologist be looking for a bizarre society to study, I would suggest he come to Ulster. It is one of Europe's oddest countries. Here, in the middle of the twentieth century, with modern technology transforming everybody's lives, you find a medieval mentality that is being dragged painfully into the eighteenth century by some forward-looking people. Anyone who belongs to the twentieth century, politically or in any other way, is a revolutionary. The attitude of the average Ulsterman can be summed up as "You'll get enough to do you." Everyone knows there are ills in our society, but if you have a job you content yourself with it and mind your own business. No criticism, no urge to go out and make progress can be afforded because these might disturb the delicate balance of the peace. Just how delicate this balance is was proved in 1968 when the civil-rights movement's demand for simple justice sent the country up in flames. Ulster is a country that has really no connections with a modern Europe. It attracts tourists who come in search of "quaint old Northern Ireland," but even in the tourist industry there is no push to make Northern Ireland worth seeing. In spite of its beautiful and fascinating countryside, it has not one top-grade hotel. The main reason for the sluggishness of our tourist industry has been the mentality of the people at the top, who weren't prepared to work in conjunction with the Irish Tourist Board over the border and sell Ireland as a whole. Most foreigners don't even know there is a border: to them Ireland is just a dog-shaped country which is emerald green. But when the Irish Tourist Board sent publicity pamphlets to America on which the border wasn't shown, the Northern Ireland Establishment kicked up hell, demanded that they be brought back, and the thin red line be drawn round the doggie's head.

Before the Treaty of 1921 put a border between Northern and Southern Ireland, Ulster comprised nine counties and was one of the four ancient kingdoms of Ireland. That treaty cut off three counties—Donegal, Cavan, and Monaghan—from the rest, and left us in the other six neither British, nor Irish, nor all of Ulster. But the history that has made us what we are goes back further than 1921. The first date that belongs to us rather than to Ireland as a whole is 1609, when thousands of Scots Presbyterians were brought over for the Plantation of Ulster. The hatred between colonized and colonizer was underlined by the difference in their religions, and the Irish were persecuted not only for being the natives, but for being Catholics as well. From then on they never quite sorted out religion from politics. After the Plantation, there were occasional Catholic rebellions, but Oliver Cromwell, once he had won the civil war in England, put an end to them. Then, in 1689, the Catholic King James II of England fled for protection to his Irish subjects before the Dutch King William of Orange, ultimately to be defeated at the

Battle of the Boyne. (According to the unreformed calendar, the Battle of the Boyne was fought on July 1, corrected to July 12 when the Gregorian calendar was introduced, and celebrated with much fervor on that day ever since.)

In the next century the system of Protestant landed gentry and oppressed Catholic peasant asserted itself, but the planter population to some extent intermarried with the natives, and there was some breakdown of religious division and the emergence of class-consciousness. Ireland's economy was already declining and vast emigrations beginning, and the Protestants were emigrating along with the Catholics. It was a Protestant, Wolfe Tone, who led the first Great Rebellion of 1798, and his movement included Catholics and Protestants fighting side by side. That rebellion, like every other rebellion in Ireland, was beaten down. The next important date was 1801, when the Act of Union began deliberately to destroy the trade of Ireland in the interests of British capitalism. The Irish linen and wool industries were run down to let the British cotton industry flourish. From then on national feeling grew, and throughout the nineteenth century there was continual struggle, punctuated by famine and emigration, to end British occupation, British imperialism, and British capitalism; and this took place throughout all Ireland.

Then came the national revolution, the Easter Rising of 1916. Now all this time the northern counties were "Orange," because a number of the people living there were descendants of the supporters of William of Orange, though many of them were against British interference and in favor of the national movement. After the failure of the Easter Rising, it was becoming obvious that the English couldn't resist Irish independence much longer, and those people who did support Britain began moving from wherever they were, scattered throughout Ireland, to the more Protestant northern counties. People began finding their own level, as it were.

However, even before the 1921 treaty created "Northern Ireland," there was a certain amount of ill-feeling between North and South, a certain readiness on the part of the southerners to sacrifice the North, because the northerners hadn't played their part in the 1916 Rising. The whole Rising was bungled: instructions were lost; there was confusion about the signal for start; an announcement appeared in a newspaper the day before the Rising saying the whole thing had been called off. It was the biggest bungle of a national revolution that any country had ever seen. And placid Ulstermen said, "Okay, there's no Rising," and stayed at home while men were slaughtered in Cork and Wexford and Dublin. So although there were disagreements about the terms of the treaty between different factions in the South, they were all quite happy to let the North go; but they saw the North as only three counties, the three most Protestant ones—County Antrim, County Down, and County Derry. These three together, along the northeast coast, couldn't have survived as a country. On the other hand, if all nine counties of Ulster had been separated from the rest of Ireland, there would have been enough national feeling in it to complete the revolution: which the pro-Britishers didn't want. So a compromise was reached, seen only as a temporary expedient on the part of the South: the new Ulster would consist of the six counties where the Protestants were the numerical majority, and things were, for a time, stable.

Some of the Protestants then decided that since the boundary had been drawn, such Catholics as remained in the North were on the wrong side of it, and should get out. The Catholics didn't want to go: down there in Eire, the Free State faction and the Republican faction were still fighting it out, and they didn't want to get involved. So here began the persecution of the Catholic working class by the Protestant working class, aided and abetted by the Northern Ireland parliament as soon as it was set up in 1921. Catholics, particularly in Belfast, were warned not to come to work; when they did come, they were thrown in the docks; Catholic homes were burned out. This immediately led to repercussions in the less Protestant counties—Fermanagh, Armagh, and Tyrone—and right into the 1930's there was religious warfare in Northern Ireland.

There are very few Christians in Northern Ireland. One American said that the most interesting thing about Holy Ireland was that its people hate each other in the name of Jesus Christ. And they do! In a country where national mentality arrests growth in every field of development, and where the average man puts up with it, the big annual excitement is July 12, the "kick the Papishes" day. You don't speak to your Catholic neighbors on the twelfth of July, nor do they speak to you. You join all the other bowler-hatte men and do the Calvary Walk.

This is the march of the Orange Order, a supposedly religious body that was founded in 1795 to keep up the traditions of Protestantism in Ulster. In fact it is a semi-religious, semi-political, totally fascist organization. All over Northern Ireland on July 12, branches of the Orange Order march off some three or four miles to a field where a meeting is held. The march signifies Christ's walk to Calvary, which didn't however happen in July, and having done this big Christian stomp, with their Bibles under their arms, they get to the field, where the respectable leaders of the organization start wallowing to the knees in Papish blood. Such is the tone of speech made from the platform. Having blasphemed their fellow Christians, they do another Christian stomp home again, get drunk, sing Orange songs, and take in the Union Jack to be put away till next year. Next day, Protestant speaks to Catholic again and community relations are back to normal. It's the same thing, but in reverse, when it comes round to the 1916 commemoration day, or to the fifteenth of August. August 15 is the feast of the Assumption of the Blessed Virgin, and what that has to do with politics nobody knows. But the Nationalists, the Catholic Tories of Northern Ireland, keep it as their day and sing anti-Orange songs, meaning every bitter word they sing.

To the Protestants, the Catholics are heretics, worshipping idols and going in for terrible pagan stuff like that. The ordinary Catholic doesn't match the Protestant in strength of feeling, but has a kind of smug attitude: "We're all Christians, but *we* are the one true church, and *they* are poor deluded brethren who will maybe know better some day. Sure the good Lord will let them into Heaven if we pray for them." But they have all forgotten the basic fundamentals of Christianity: Love your enemy?—not at all! They rationalize it by saying the people they disapprove of are the enemies of God, thereby justifying their hatred of people who never did them any harm.

Both the Protestant Unionists and the Catholic Nationalists deny they discriminate against each other, but both use religion to divide and rule the working class. It is only less serious on the Catholic side because there are fewer Catholic bosses and fewer Catholic local authorities in a position to practice discrimination. It is a tactic that has made the ruling minority look like a majority and has kept the Unionist Party in power since Northern Ireland's inception. Polarized by this ploy into their religious sects, and set against each other, the ordinary people have not been able to combine and fight politically for their real interests. At the bottom of the social pyramid with nothing to lose, the Catholic working man doesn't really fear the Protestant; but the Protestant working man, who has very little, feels the need to hang on to his Protestant identity in case he loses what little he has. He fears the Catholic because he knows that any gain made by the Catholic minority will be his loss, for the businessmen and the landowners, Orange or Nationalist, are not going to suffer losses on anybody's behalf. Where discrimination hurts most is in employment and housing. You come to a factory looking for a job and they ask you which school you went to. If its name was "Saint Somebody," they know you are a Catholic and you don't get taken on. Until the civil-rights campaign forced a promise of reform, housing was *the* burning issue in Northern Ireland, because only householders have a vote in local elections: subtenants, lodgers, and adult children living at home are all without the vote, and thus a quarter of the electorate is disenfranchised (until, as the government now promises, 1971). So it is very important where you build houses and for whom you build them. Too many houses for Catholics could upset the majority on a Protestant council, or vice versa. The policy in both the Protestant-run councils, which are the majority, and the few Catholic-run councils, is to control the way the votes go by having separate housing estates for people of different religions, and by awarding tenancies in the interests of political dominance.

At ground level, this means that you grow up very much within your own circle, not meeting people of the other religion until you have left school and gone to work or university, and not on the whole intermarrying because you only marry those you meet.

I went to a very militantly Republican grammar school and, under its influence, began to revolt against the Establishment, on the simple rule of thumb, highly satisfying to a ten-year-old, that Irish equals good, English equals bad. At the age of twelve I made my first political protest. I decided to enter a talent competition which for some reason or other was being organized in Cookstown. Most of the members of my family are quite talented. My eldest sister, Mary, now a nun, paints a little, but her main gift is for making something out of nothing. When she was a child our house was coming down with Japanese gardens: there would be clay all over the place, and bits of twig, and an old biscuit tin, and suddenly there was a Japanese garden. I'm useless at that sort of thing. She used to write what I, as a younger sister, thought was excellent poetry, but unfortunately she took it all off with her to the convent. Marie is talented in an entirely different way: she does the ordinary things that everyone does, like sewing and knitting and embroidery, but in half the time and twice as well as anyone else, and she cooks brilliantly. Elizabeth is musically talented; she's a very good pianist. Elizabeth, Paddy, and myself all sing, and I'm considered the best singer because I've got the loudest voice. As children we often used to perform either for visitors or at children's concerts, but we were not encouraged to consider ourselves talented children: my mother squashed any tendencies toward conceit.

When I was in my first year at grammar school, I had a long-playing record, "The Rebel," on which the actor

Michael MacLiammoir recited the works of Padraig Pearse, one of the martyrs of 1916. I thought it was great stuff, and played it over and over again, and the more I listened to it the more convinced I became that although MacLiammoir had put it over as a work of art, he had failed to convey the true emotion of a patriot saying what he felt. Anyway I learned three pieces from the record for the three heats of the talent competition, and they were all very militant. "The Rebel" ends:

"I say to the master of my people 'Beware the risen people who will take what you would not give!' "

Another piece I chose was "The Fool," which has this passage:

"But the fools, the fools! They have left us our Fenian dead! While Ireland holds these graves, Ireland unfree will never be at rest."

And my third and final choice was Robert Emmett's speech from the dock before his execution in 1804.

Well, off I went and recited this fighting stuff at the talent competition, and I recited it well, went through the three heats, and won first prize. Cookstown was outraged. During the three weeks of the competition, the horror grew. "Imagine a daughter of Lizzie Devlin having the cheek to go down there and say a thing like that! That comes from her father's side of the family." I believe I won on merit, but the general townspeople said I had blackmailed the judges, who were local businessmen and so forth, into awarding me first prize because I could have accused them of bigotry if they hadn't. Feeling got very high and on the last day I had to have a police escort home to protect me from the people who would otherwise have given me a cuff on the ear for my impudence. My mother was delighted; she was somewhat embarrassed, but secretly glad and proud that at least I had enough of my father in me to go somewhere I was hated and look people straight in the face. This was a gift both my parents had: they never shied away uncomfortably from company they knew rejected them. As well as showing courage and defiance, I had won £10 and this too was welcome at home. To me it was like £100. I'd got the average weekly wage of a man in Northern Ireland just for standing up and saying a wee bit of prose. A year or two later, from the same feeling of defiance, I wore a tricolor pin in my coat, precisely because the Northern Ireland Flags and Emblems Act forbade it. Only once did a policeman ask me to remove it. "You remove it," I said, but as his hand came out to take the badge, I added: "If you touch me without a warrant, I'll have you in court for assault!" He just laughed and said, "Go on there, you troublemaker!" I trotted on, feeling very proud I had won, but once I'd discovered I could get away with it, I lost interest in the badge.

I went to school from the age of three and a half, to begin with in Miss Murray's nursery school, held in the front parlor of her home in Chapel Street, Cookstown. My primary school was St. Brigid's Convent, Cookstown, a big gray building, with high ceilings and partitioned rooms. A chestnut tree overshadowed the playground, a place I principally remember for having suffered there the torture of organized games. St. Brigid's was run by the Sisters of Mercy and was part primary school, for those going on to grammar school, and part commercial school for the others. The grammar-school potential got special treatment to rush us through examinations, but we were excluded from the music and sewing and cooking classes. As a result we are among the clumsiest, most useless females ever God produced, whereas our non-grammar-school contemporaries from St. Brigid's are some of the handiest.

I went from Miss Murray's into the first grade at St. Brigid's, where I stayed for a year, then straight into the third grade and rapidly into the fourth. There the school inspector found me, not only very small but also very young, and I was kept in the fourth grade another year before I was allowed to take the exam for grammar school. This almost turned out to be the end of my school career. I had always had a bad attendance record, because I was so often ill, and that year, when I was supposed to be absorbing masses of intelligence tests, square roots, and so forth, I was off with asthma every second week. The nuns used to come down to the house: "Get her out of bed! There's an exam to be passed!" I wasn't particularly worried whether I went to grammar school or not, but I passed the examination, to everybody's surprise.

St. Patrick's Academy, Dungannon, where I then went, was a militantly Republican school, and it owed its fiery partisan slant to the vice-principal, Mother Benignus, whom we called Reverend Mother, and who is, among the people who have influenced me, one of those I most respect. To Mother Benignus everything English was bad. She *hated* the English —and with good reason: her entire family had suffered at the hands of the British forces. Everything we did in school was Irish-oriented. She was a fanatic about Irish culture, which was all right for people like me who were also fanatical about it, but which did drive lots of people away from it who couldn't take Irish culture for breakfast, dinner, and tea. She didn't hate Protestants, but her view was that you couldn't very well put up with them, they weren't Irish, and that clinched the argument. When I was a senior, the school produced a netball team that could have beaten any netball team in the North of Ireland, but Mother Benignus wouldn't let it play Protestant schools on the grounds that we might have to stand for the National Anthem and it would be embarrassing. We told her, "Mother, it wouldn't be embarrassing at all: we would stand. Then we'd invite them over here, and play 'The Soldier's Song' and they would stand too. It would be just a matter of politeness." But she wasn't to be persuaded.

We learned Irish history. People who went to Protestant schools learned British history. We were all learning the same things, the same events, the same period of time, but the interpretations we were given were very different. At the state school they teach that the Act of Union was brought about to help strengthen the trade agreements between England and Ireland. We were taught that it was a malicious attempt to bleed Ireland dry of her linen industry, which was affecting English cotton. We learned our Irish history from *Fallon's Irish History Aids*, Fallon's being a publishing firm in Southern Ireland. Now the Ministry of Education had issued a memorandum saying that *Fallon's Irish History Aids* were not to be used in schools, because they were no more than sedition and treason in the name of history. On a point of principle, *all* our books were published by Fallon's. When the Ministry wrote to complain, Mother Benignus wrote back in Irish, just to make another point clear.

We were a very voluntary voluntary school, under the minimum control of the government, and occasionally offers would come of more financial help in exchange for a greater government say in the school. Officers would come from the

Ministry of Education, and argue: "Look, if you come under government control, you'll get another 20 per cent grant." And they would be chased off the premises. Immediately a mass movement would start to raise enough money to produce the necessary facility before the Ministry inspector came back. All our days were spent organizing concerts or raffles or draws or competitions to raise the money to get more equipment for the lab, or a new cooker in the kitchen, or for resurfacing the tennis court. This is where it was a good school. It had a good academic reputation, though socially it wasn't a good school: it did not attract the better class of citizen. There was very little discipline and it didn't produce people who took an active part in the community; but at least in our struggle to do without government help and interference, we ended up appreciating things much better than if they had been forced on us.

I knew no Irish when I went to grammar school, but the class I joined was a class of crude political rebels: we knew nothing about politics except what we were for and against, and we were for Ireland and Mother Benignus was our heroine. In addition to our passion for Ireland, we had a very good teacher of Gaelic, with an enthusiastic approach to the subject, so that at the end of my first year the whole class was way above the standard of Irish-speaking expected of eleven-year-olds. Each year the Gael Linn, an organization which exists to preserve the Irish language, sponsors a school competition in Northern Ireland and awards a shield to the school with the best Irish-conversation standard and a scholarship to the best individual pupil. At the end of my first year, our school won the shield and I won the scholarship, and when the shield was presented, special mention was made of my class, which had been partly responsible for the award. Since I was the best of the best who had helped to win the shield, I became the darling of Mother Benignus's life and a protégée to be sent to the stars ever afterwards. I got away with murder in that school on the basis of my heart being in the right place. Each year an Irish drama festival was held in the locality, and other things being equal we were allowed to go to it on Wednesday afternoon. One particular year the program looked very good: it was getting away from the old Irish kitchen-sink drama and presenting plays in translation, such as those of Chekhov. So three of us organized a large-scale truancy and about twenty pupils sat watching plays for three whole days. With twenty of us missing school, Mother Benignus knew perfectly well where we were. She also knew who was responsible. But when the festival was over and we turned up in school once more, she merely said, "I hope you benefited greatly, and that you will keep your enthusiasm in *reasonable* bounds in the future."

When I first joined St. Patrick's Academy, I was a very timid, terrified person. The other girls all seemed to be independent toughies. Their general attitude was: "We know you have to wear your berets coming to school in the morning; that's why we carry them in our pockets." I was so scared of them that I asked to leave the room when the teacher left, so I could get away from them. But my success in Gaelic and the prominence this gave me in the school cured me of that. The combined effect of Mother Benignus and my fellow students turned me into a convinced Republican, and a year of absorbing the lesson, "We are Irish. We are proud of our history, our dead, our culture, and our language," groomed me for the talent competition.

Mother Benignus was a very kind-hearted woman. Financially the school was never what it should have been because when it came to the paying of fees, if you didn't have the money, you didn't pay. It was written off, or held over, and she would just say, "Well, we'll work a bit harder and make up for it." She was a good kind of socialist. She imposed a capital fee to cover the school's expenses on all qualified pupils—the ones getting scholarships from the state, that is; it came to one guinea a term, which of course everybody could afford, and so she collected one guinea a term from all the people who didn't have to pay to make up the deficit of the children who had neither scholarships nor the money for fees. When we got into unreasonable debt, we just held another competition.

But she was narrow-minded. She couldn't bear, for instance, to see women in masculine attire: wearing jeans was disgusting, she said. And knocking around with the scruffy boys in the boys' academy next door was just a total disgrace. This was amusing enough when you were young, but as you got older it became tiresome to feel her eagle eye upon you when you wanted to walk to the bus stop with some reasonably handsome male. She never missed anything, and you would be hauled over the coals next morning: "You were seen eating crisps out of a bag in the street! Have you no self-respect?" Sucking lollipops in the street was considered sinking to the depths of degradation, and the punishment for these things was quite severe; they merited lengthy tellings-off. But if you knocked somebody halfway down the stairs, you wouldn't get a blessing on your work; it was very un-Christian; you had better apologize, and that was that.

When I was a senior pupil our group resented the fact that we didn't have a common room to ourselves, so we took over a small library where we studied and made ourselves at home. We smuggled in a kettle and a jar of instant coffee and some cups and hid them in the library cupboard. When the bell rang for break and everybody was supposed to go outside for fresh air, we locked the library door and made coffee. And talked. We didn't gossip about other girls in the school or make cynical remarks about the teachers; instead, we analyzed the situation in Northern Ireland and discussed why most of us were going to leave it. I was one of the few who didn't plan to leave Northern Ireland. But the only possible future the others could see was either to get a university education and leave Northern Ireland or go to a Catholic training college and become a Catholic teacher in a Catholic school. None of us wanted to be Catholic teachers —and none of us wanted to be nuns. This was a big drama in the school: for something like fifteen years they hadn't produced a nun from the school, until my sister went and broke the record—and was I disgraced! They wanted about six of us to enter the convent, and we had to fight them off tooth and nail.

Anyway, one day when we were dissecting Northern Ireland behind the locked doors of the library, a general assembly was called. I was head girl at that time and should have called it, but when we got to the assembly hall things were already in progress. It was a uniform inspection—one of many—held this time because girls' gym tunics were getting disgracefully shorter with every passing day. So there was a crisis on, and we had missed it. When we made our appearance, Mother Benignus demanded: "Where have you been? And what have you been discussing?"

One of my friends, Bernadette O'Neill, who was about the most militant person I knew at school, roared from the back of the hall: "Politics, Mother. We have been discussing politics!"

"And if," said Mother Benignus, standing up, "the senior girls of this school have nothing better to discuss than politics, I suggest they should be working. Politics is a waste of time." And she the most political person in the school!

I was head girl at that time by popular acclaim, and the next year I was elected head girl by the prefects. Mother Benignus didn't want me to be head girl the second year: she thought it was making me swell-headed and that I was taking over the school from under her feet. In fact there were three of us—Aideen Mallon, Sheila O'Farrell, and myself. For two years we made ourselves responsible for behavior in the school and in that time took it from the brink of chaos and made of it a reasonably civilized society. The nuns weren't prepared to cane anybody: their attitude was we should behave ourselves for the greater honor and glory of God. But delinquent juveniles didn't work on those assumptions, and there was very little discipline or respect for one's betters in the school. Aideen, Sheila, and I created our own detention period. We used to make children stay in after school and anyone who broke the silence merely prolonged the detention period by another three minutes. The extra three minutes were totted up on the blackboard, and sometimes we were there for an hour and a half. Another complaint was that girls didn't change from their heavy outdoor shoes into their indoor shoes, and they were damaging the school floors. We put a guard on the cloakroom: any girl who forgot to bring indoor shoes was made to go in her stocking feet. After about three days of that, people generally discovered that it wasn't hard to remember their indoor shoes. So we built up our little syndicate of Stalinism, which only lasted a few weeks, for all that was necessary was to impose discipline in the first place. We made the school something more than an academic machine by producing a debating society and a netball team, and we widened its interests from exclusively Irish culture to English-speaking drama and debates.

Because it was the kind of school it was, the history teacher, Mrs. Bradley, was Stalin in disguise. Outside the classroom, she was a very friendly, enthusiastic kind of person, but inside the classroom her system of teaching was to thump everything down your throat. "That's it! Learn it! Or out against the wall!" You had to stand up without moving until such time as your brain registered that which it should have registered; or, if you hadn't learned it in the first place, until you gave in and admitted it. But anything she taught you, you never forgot. She came to us in the library one day for help. She had a particularly stupid class, and even her thump-on-the-head-with-a-book, out-against-the-wall, and stand-till-you-drop tactics had failed to get anything into these kids' brains. She decided a bit of the education touch wouldn't do any harm, and so she planned to produce a wall chart and asked us to make it for her. It was to cover the junior history course, which included most of British history from the Stuarts to the Battle of Waterloo.

We got the junior class working to bring us in pictures of all the important British kings and heroes and generals they could find, and we gathered up old encyclopedias and history books, and with all the material we made a good, colorful, lucid chart, showing who was who and what they had done in the fewest words possible. To head it off, we took a page from an educational magazine that showed a picture of Nelson under the caption, "They fought for their coun-

Benignus storming up after me. At the top of the stairs we stopped and the argument began again, with Mother Benignus claiming she wasn't a bigot, but a patriot. My favorite habit at that time was waving my finger, so I waved my finger at her and said, "Mother, you are one of the greatest bigots I have ever met!" She had a ruler in her hand and she practically took my finger off with it. She was beaten. She just said, "Don't wave your finger at the principal of this school!"

I had called her a bigot, I had walked out without being dismissed, I had closed the door in her face, I had forced her to walk up the stairs after me. But she knew I was right, and all she said was, "Don't wave your finger at me." The chart went back up. Mrs. Bradley stayed, and there has been a love-hate relationship between Mother Benignus and myself ever since. Although I have outgrown her politics, Mother Benignus will always have my admiration and affection, because she is the most truly charitable person I have known. Her heart is in the right place.

Chapter 5

Politics for me meant debate, not action, when I joined Queen's University, Belfast, in October 1965. I was perfectly aware of the injustices in Northern Ireland's society, but I had a sort of consciously virtuous attitude to the whole problem: at least it would make no difference to me personally whether someone was a Catholic or a Protestant. This impartiality wasn't difficult to achieve, for I never knew what my friends' religion was, or whether they had any at all. I come from a very strong Catholic background myself, but it was also strongly Christian, and it is the Christian element in my background that keeps me in the Catholic Church. On the principle "Tell me your company and I'll tell you who you are," I might very well reflect that I don't care for the company which the Catholic Church keeps, and clear off. But I make a distinction between the doctrines of the Church, which matter, and the structure invented by half a dozen Italians who got to be pope and which is of very little use to anybody. It doesn't worry me if half the clergy trot off to get married, because that wouldn't alter the essential Church, which is still, for me, the best manifestation of my Christian beliefs. Growing up in Cookstown, however, leads to cynicism about the "good Catholic." "Good Catholic" and "practicing Catholic" are terms I hate: as far as I am concerned they are labels suggesting how good a hypocrite you are, how well you go through the ritual. You are an exemplary Catholic if you go to Mass every day and tear your neighbors asunder on the way home from church, but the really charitable people who don't go to Mass on Sundays are heathen, and you are quite entitled to look down your pious nose at them and say, "Disgrace to their country!" For to be Irish is to be Catholic in the conservative mind. We say the family rosary because in the penal days it was the rosary that saved us from Cromwell. And that's the reason some people have for belonging to a church!

As are many other aspects of Irish society, the Catholic Church there is ultraconservative. To be quite cruel about it, Irish Catholics are more interested in the rosary beads than in the rosary—which, for those not familiar with it, is a series of meditations on the life, death, and resurrection of Jesus Christ. They are not interested in the *reasons* for doing things. The Church is falling apart at the prospect of its no longer being an obligation to go to Mass on Sundays. It is as important not to eat meat on Fridays as it is to believe in the Holy Trinity. Everything is blindly accepted from the pope down to the parish priest: "That's our orders."

Among the best traitors Ireland has ever had, Mother Church ranks at the very top, a massive obstacle in the path to equality and freedom. She has been a force for conservatism, not on the basis of preserving Catholic doctrine or preventing the corruption of her children, but simply to ward off threats to her own security and influence. The Church indirectly—because of the parish priest and his position in the small town, and what-the-bishop-says-is-law—is very influential. She is more powerful in the South of Ireland than in the North, and there her power more than somewhat tends to corrupt her. You have bishops there who own land, who make a profit out of owning land, and who flog it to others to make a profit out of.

In the Protestant North, the Church is not so obviously a part of the Establishment, but it would never come out and support a clash with the government. In the North the churches, Catholic and Protestant, should have been campaigning for the dignity of the people years and years ago. They never did. They should have been making some effort to break down religious sectarianism in the country. They did nothing. Very few sermons have I heard preached on tolerance of people who have different views from you. Occasionally there is a sermon saying that whether you like it or not, you should honor your father and your mother and your legally appointed boss, and not complain about how they treat you. But when the Church sees the initiative against injustice being taken by somebody else, she becomes afraid that her influence is slipping and condemns the initiative as trouble-making with which no good Catholic should have anything to do.

I went up to university with some vague notion of being able, one day, to improve some aspect of life in Northern Ireland. In my last years at school I had toyed with the idea of becoming a teacher for the gypsies, and later I thought of joining either the Ministry of Health and Social Services or the Ministry of Education, to work from within the citadel. But it seemed a long process, waiting to get into a position where I could have an impact on the system. Without any clear idea of what I planned to do with it, I started an

Honours Celtic degree course. It seemed a natural choice: Celtic had been my best subject at school, and I was very interested in all the Celtic languages—from a cultural, not a political, point of view. I joined the Irish Democratic Club at Queen's, which trotted round the country to festivals and competitions, producing plays in the Irish language. But my main interest was in the Gaelic Society, which held Irish debates. Very soon I became irritated by the Gaelic Society. It was a small, inward-looking group, making very little attempt to reach anybody outside the converted, and boring people like myself to death. We produced an Irish-language newspaper called *An Scathan* (The Reflection), and there were eternal arguments over articles printed in it, over who was editor, over failures to sell the newspaper, over the fact that pamphlets and papers sent by organizations in the South hadn't been distributed by the society. In my second year at Queen's, when I gave up Celtic Studies in favor of Psychology, I became secretary of the Gaelic Society, and at the end of that year I resigned my office and my membership with a disillusioned farewell speech: until such time as they were interested in culture as culture, instead of who was leader of the group, I was bailing out.

However I was still keen on debating and used to attend meetings of the "Literific"—the Literary and Scientific Society—which organized debates just for the fun of debating, not to press any point of view, political or otherwise. In its day, the Literific had been a good forum for discussion, but by 1965 it had degenerated into nothing more than student obscenity. You could get up and shout, "Spit on the Vice-Chancellor!" without any further explanation, and be sure of applause. My friends enjoyed this frivolity but I didn't, and I never spoke at a Queen's debate in my first year. My second year saw the birth of the Union Debating Society. I had no hand in its formation, but I was one of many who saw in it a chance of discussing something worth talking about. I should have liked serious discussion on such subjects as the university structure, the relations between student and lecturer, or between student and tutor. The most obvious thing about the tutorials I attended was the credibility gap between the idea that this was an informal discussion group and the respectful attitude of the students toward the tutor. The relationship was one of teacher and pupil, there was no equal communication of ideas, and people accepted that what the lecturers said should be reproduced in examinations.

The first debate I spoke at was on the motion: Free love is too expensive. As far as I was concerned, this could be treated with a certain amount of humor, but it was a serious subject of concern to every student present. However, it degenerated into a lot of double-meaning jokes on the comparative cost of prostitutes in Amsterdam and San Francisco and about the price of contraceptives on the black market in Southern Ireland, making it cheaper to conduct your affairs in Ulster. Everybody thought it was just so amusing. Well, I sat through this for about two hours, until I couldn't resist standing up any longer, and then I told them that not only were they ignorant of the basic sexual morality of their own society, but they were also still so much part of their environment that they were incapable of rising above the situation and looking at it without embarrassment: hence all the bravado and the doubtful jokes. My own opinion was, I said, that while society had a double attitude, tolerating free love but not tolerating illegitimate children, free love *was* too expensive. We should be talking about the moral and social cost of individual independence and we were talking about contraceptives. I proposed that the motion should not be put until every student had gone out and troubled to learn a bit more about the society he or she was living in.

Everybody felt very uncomfortable when I accused them of ignorance of their own sexual morality, but when I used the word "bastard," the tension was broken, and this so-called intellectual gathering came down in an uproar of laughing and giggling. I finished off my speech by saying, "You may find the word bastard amusing. You may find free love is not expensive, if in fact it can be had for two-and-ninepence in Sandy Row [a poor area of Belfast]. But how many people here can stand up without blushing and say without any qualms on the matter, 'I am a bastard'?" Nobody stood up and everything went dead quiet. Then tittering broke out and several people stood up and said, "I am a bastard." Finally a young fellow got up. "It is quite obvious," he said, "that none of those people has ever seriously been called a bastard. I have, and I understand the point you are making." But the debate broke up because people couldn't face serious discussion on it. Such was the mentality of Queen's at the time: people consciously played at being students, carrying briefcases about and looking intellectual.

Over the course of my first two years at university, I attended meetings of all the political parties. I felt I needed some ideology, so off I went on my round of the parties in search of one. There was then at Queen's a Tory Club, the Young Liberals, the Labour group that had risen and fallen over the years, the National Democrats, who were a new group, and the Young Socialists, who weren't actually part of the university at all. They were all little gatherings of initiates, but there was also the New Ireland Society, which was large and loosely structured, attracting people of different tendencies. In none of the political parties could I find anything to believe in. They all had a sort of self-importance, as if their interest in politics raised them above the level of ordinary people, and they all went in for an intellectual type of discussion that had no relevance to any kind of society I knew. They tried to be very sophisticated, working out policies and inviting guest speakers down; but they weren't *real*. You got the impression that they really didn't care what went on outside the university, so long as they had plenty to talk about. There was more real politics in the Folk Music Society than in any of the parties. They sang black civil-rights songs in the Folk Music Society before anybody else in Queen's was interested in the race problem, and they were singing songs about unemployment in Belfast long before the civil-rights movement took it up. That was a good society. It had a strong American influence in it, but because of this there was another section that was determined to keep Irish influence, so you had the best of both American prote..ongs and traditional Irish folk music.

What made student politics all the more absurd at that time was that Queen's was basically a nine-to-six university. None of us was the kind of independent, twenty-four-hours-a-day student that you get at colleges in England. We went home for tea. You were a student during the day, but your mother asked you where you were going at eight o'clock at night.

For a moment in my third year, it looked as if there might be some excitement. The Minister of Home Affairs issued an order banning Republican Clubs. These had been allowed to continue throughout Northern Ireland, though the Republican Party itself had always been illegal. Immediately the ban was announced, a Republican Club was formed in Queen's and I joined it. We had a peaceful little demonstration against the ban, carried a coffin to the Minister's house, mourned the death of democracy and so forth, and went back to the university. But then the steam went out of the Republican Club. It didn't seem to have anything other than an existence.

So, disenchanted with Queen's politics, I moved to the do-good organizations. These were Catholic societies who visited the poor, decorated houses for old people, did voluntary work at hospitals, and so on. I stayed with them for a while until I decided they were just perpetuating aspects of the system I didn't like. When we visited old people in their homes, we were letting off the neighbors and relatives who should have done it and who, instead of saying, "Those people are doing it—why don't we?" were saying, "Those people are doing it—we don't need to." By carol-singing at Christmas to collect money for coal for poor families, we were relieving the local authorities of their responsibility. They just budgeted our contribution into what they spent and cut down on their own spending.

For a while after that I wandered about by myself, making terrorist plans. I've often wondered why the IRA is so keen on blowing up bridges, when Northern Ireland offers much greater possibilities for disruption and international publicity. In Derry there is an American communications base that is used as a look-out post for the rest of Europe and whose strategic importance has never been appreciated by people in Northern Ireland. This base, it seemed to me, was custom-built for causing an international crisis and bringing Northern Ireland to the attention of the world, and I developed a very nasty plan for its destruction. The first thing to do was to set fire to Gortin Forest Park in County Tyrone. It always closes in the evening, so nobody would be in it by about nine o'clock at night, and since it is in the middle of the wilderness, you wouldn't endanger any houses. Once Gortin Forest Park was burning nicely, all the fire brigades in Ulster would come storming around to deal with it, blaming the IRA; and while everybody was putting out that fire, you could set fire to Tullamore Forest Park on the other side of the country. With the entire country running around putting out fires it would take no more than half a dozen hand grenades lobbed over the wall of the communications base to create a very nasty diplomatic incident. It would involve the British, because this was British territory and they were supposed to be guarding it. It would involve the Americans, because it belonged to them. And it would raise the question of why the United States had a base in Northern Ireland at all.

I never told anybody this idea because, quite honestly, it terrified me. As theoretical terrorism, it was great, but I couldn't reconcile myself to the thought that maybe, against all the probabilities, someone might be in Gortin Forest Park when it went up in flames. Another idea I had was to send an ultimatum to every fly-by-night foreign firm who invested money in Northern Ireland, giving them a breakdown of the short-term profits to them, and the long-term inefficiency to us, of their operation. Such firms are attracted to Northern Ireland by government building grants and short-term tax concessions. But when the tax concessions run out, so do they, leaving behind an empty factory and another couple of hundred unemployed. I planned to send them a warning: "You have three years to promise you will remain here more than ten years, or we'll blow your little factory out of the ground." Those were my militant Republican days. But I got over these dreams of violence, and told myself it didn't matter if the people who kept us in poverty were called

British or not. It wasn't simply getting Britain out of Ireland that mattered: it was the fact that we were economically depressed, and I couldn't see terrorism solving that.

My mother died in January 1967. She was forty-six. I was home on vacation from Belfast when she decided after Christmas that she just couldn't go on and went to bed. Elizabeth and I said she must go to hospital. She was terrified of going. "If I go to hospital, I'll never come out," she said. It was the first time I'd ever seen her afraid, and it frightened me, but I reacted brutally: "Don't lie there feeling sorry for yourself—you'll never get well unless you go to hospital." She went, but she was right all the time.

At the hospital it was discovered that she had cancer and the doctors decided to operate, although her weight, her weak heart, and her general physical condition were against it. When the operation was over, it was generally pronounced a success, and I alone was told by the doctor that in fact the growth had been too far developed to be removed entirely, and my mother had no more than a year to live. Everyone else was in high spirits. Although my mother was only forty-six, she had looked sixty, with her white face and gray hair. In hospital, with all the glucose and the blood transfusions and the medical attention, she looked as she should have done at forty-six. She actually had rosy cheeks and bright eyes, and everybody was feeling optimistic. Meanwhile I was wondering whom, if anybody, I could tell. I couldn't tell Marie or any of the others because they would have just gone mad, and my eldest sister, Mary, who was the natural person to tell, was in the convent in Norfolk at the time. I didn't know if she would be allowed home, if I wrote to her, and I suspected that if she was forbidden to come, she would just come anyway.

While I was in this indecision, I called one afternoon at the hospital, and found my mother very happy and contented and resigned. This alarmed me. We'd recently been having arguments, she and I, about religion and about my attitude to people who came to visit her. "I wonder where the hell they were, all your life," I'd say. "Bloody hypocrites! People like that would drive you out of the Church!" She feared that I was in fact drifting away from the Church, so I thought she would be pleased when I told her that afternoon that I'd called at the Redemptorist Church in Clonard. In this church there is a shrine to Our Lady of Perpetual Succour, who was always a favorite patron of the family. But my mother just didn't seem to mind about it any more.

On my way home that evening I went to see my Uncle Tom, who was engaged at this time to the girl nursing my mother, and I asked him if he thought my mother was dying. He blew his top at me for going round making alarmist statements, so I went home and sat up all night thinking, Shall I ring Mary in Norfolk and tell her to come home? Or find someone to take me back to the hospital? Or go back to Tom again? But in the end I just sat there, and I was still in the armchair at eight o'clock next morning when someone knocked on the back door. I unlocked it, and there was Tom. I was very angry with what my relatives did that night. Apparently my mother had taken very ill about eleven o'clock, and the nurse had telephoned Tom. In the course of that night every relative who had ever turned their back on my mother was notified, but no one came out to tell us till my mother told Tom to come. Anyway, here he was at last, with my mother's orders: we were all to get up, go to Mass and Communion, and then to the hospital.

At the hospital everybody was running around organizing who should be told that my mother was very ill. When I said, "Did anyone ring Mary?" the reaction was, "Why ring her? She's in the convent." So *I* telephoned. Mary had been sitting there waiting for someone to tell her to come home, and she came immediately. By the time she arrived at five o'clock that Sunday evening, my mother had just died. At the moment when she actually died, the only people in the room were a priest, my Aunt Mary, and myself. All the organizers had drifted off to find something else to do.

Then everybody broke down and cried and said, "She was a great woman." And to keep myself from telling them all to clear off to Hell, I set about getting in touch with the undertaker and arranging for the funeral. Then there was the first argument: my mother's remains should be brought home. I said they weren't ever going home—they were going straight from the hospital to the church. But what about all the people who would want to come to the house and pay their respects? "She was alive for forty-six years," I said. "They had ample opportunity to come." It was the same thing all over again as at my father's funeral. Mrs. Heaney's daughter was being buried and the town turned out to do homage. I was very callous about the burying of Mrs. Heaney's daughter, and from my point of view all the wrong people were there. Nobody rang Uncle Sammy. But if I couldn't stop people attending the funeral, I could stop them coming into our home. When they said, "I came to offer you my condolences on the death of your mother," I replied, "Thank you very much, it's very kind of you," and closed the door. And people thought I was a hard bitch.

At my mother's death, our family just paralyzed itself. Quite disgustingly we lived on brandy. We got up in the morning, sat around the house in a daze all day, and couldn't sleep when it came to nighttime. Since none of them drank, it occurred to me that the only thing to do was to feed them brandy and sleeping tablets. This knocked us out and we went to bed and slept till morning, then got up again for another day of sitting about. And that went on for three solid weeks, with Elizabeth breaking the monotony by crying all day and Marie by crying all night, even in her sleep. I don't think I shed one solitary tear for about six weeks after my mother died: somebody had to run the household. And Paddy was quite sane. But John was literally hysterical. He found everything funny. His entire repertoire of dubious Irish jokes was told repeatedly, day in, day out, and such respectable people as got through my guard to come and mourn found themselves sitting around laughing, because the jokes were funny.

People bustled in and out and tried to help, and this was when our Protestant friend and neighbor was especially good to us. By the time I had the breakfast made in the morning, she would have cleaned the whole house: she just did it and disappeared again, because she knew it was neither the time nor the place to start talking. When it was getting near dinnertime, she would come over with a great pot of dinner she had cooked, and simply leave it there for me to serve out. This is why it was so unbelievable to find her standing there in the street, screaming abuse at me later on.

So we struggled on. Mary went back to the convent and Marie began running the house. Elizabeth was doing her A-level examinations that year, to come up to the university in the autumn, and Paddy was doing O-levels. John was at secondary school in Cookstown. I should have gone back to the university, but it never occurred to me that I should explain to my professor that I was taking a couple of months off. Some time at the beginning of March 1967, I reappeared at Queen's and was summoned to the professor's office. "And where have you been since the beginning of term?" he asked. It all seemed such a matter of fact to me that I just said, "My mother died." The professor was all sympathy and concern: he patched up my academic failings for me, told me I needed a week's rest, and suggested I come and see him again in a week's time.

I had a subsidiary English examination to face that summer and should have been studying for it. But I couldn't buckle down to work. I was living then with four other girls in a house in Rugby Avenue, Belfast, and I would waken about six o'clock in the morning and lie there thinking about getting up till eleven o'clock. Then I took my briefcase to the Psychology Department, left it there, and went out again to walk round and round the Botanic Gardens till lunchtime. I met my friends; into the library with them, swearing I would work; out again to the Botanic Gardens or downtown. I must have walked every street in Belfast—not thinking, just plodding round and round. The professor called me in again: "There's really no point in your being only physically present," he said. "If you want time I'll see that you get it." All I really wanted was to get finished with the university: what was the point of an Honours Psychology degree when my only possible future was going back to Cookstown to teach and look after the others?

With the passage of time after my mother's death the family was going more and more to pieces. Marie was like an automaton: if someone told her to cook or shop, she cooked and shopped. If no one drew her attention to the fact it was dinnertime and there was nothing to eat, she just didn't notice. Elizabeth, in her last year at school, was trying to keep things organized and failing completely. She was almost on the point of mental breakdown: the tap dripping was people calling her; she could see my mother coming round corners. Paddy, who was seventeen, had got to the stage of weeping nonstop. John took the same escape route as me—he stayed in bed, but he couldn't accept the idea that what had been his home was now somewhere to get fed and lodged. Then the relatives decided they would sort us out. They suggested that, since no one could take all of us, we should be divided among our aunts and uncles.

This plan brought the family to their senses. We had a little meeting, and I said, "Look, if we don't pull ourselves together, we're going to be sawn apart by well-meaning relatives." We agreed we would struggle on until May when the university year finished, and I would decide over the summer whether to drop the Honours Psychology course and finish as quickly as possible or whether to stay on at the university. We had the summer at home to readjust in and we got into a good working routine.

In October 1967 Elizabeth joined me at Queen's. Marie, John, and Paddy lived at home, and Elizabeth and I traveled back to Cookstown on weekends. This worked out all right—except for John. He still felt he was living in a hotel, and his solution was to leave school and make his own world. He was only fifteen and nobody would allow him to leave school, but he just stopped going: he walked out of the front door on his way to school in the morning, and in the back door five minutes later. Marie knew what was going on, but she felt sorry for him and shielded him. I knew nothing about it until his headmaster wrote to me, as John's legal guardian: "Are you aware that it is three weeks since John appeared at school? Please send a medical certificate if he is ill, or call and see me if he is playing truant." John would go back to school only on the condition that he was allowed to quit the academic stream and join the technical stream. To his mind, the academic stream led only to further dreary years at school, followed by teacher's training college or university, and he wanted none of it. He wanted to start looking for a decent trade right away. I said fair enough; I'd put it to the headmaster. The headmaster told me he couldn't possibly allow a moment's whim to destroy a career: John was suffering emotional stress at the moment, but he would regret it later. To complicate matters, the headmaster and the entire school had been very lenient with John, letting him get away with enormities because of my mother's death, and he resented this special treatment. He began breaking school rules to force them to forget he was an orphan and start caning him as they would anybody else. Finally these tactics worked. The headmaster took him by the two shoulders and shook him till the teeth rattled in his head, and said: "Look, you can come back here; you can go into the technical stream; but if you put one foot wrong, I'll be waiting for you! If you fail your technical exams, don't think you're getting out of school: you will be back in the grammar stream, you will take the grammar school exams, and you will pass them!"

So that was the school problem solved, but John still found his home too empty, and to make some sort of stabilizing center for him I decided in January 1968 to live in Cookstown and travel daily to the university in Belfast. The worst thing about it was having to get up at half past six. It was winter, it was still dark, and I fell into every puddle in the dark on my way to the other end of town to catch the bus. But at least we had breakfast together in the morning and tea together at night, and John was much happier. It worked pretty well, except that Bernadette was getting gradually grayer with every passing day. Life improved a little when Northern Ireland's first motorway was completed, which made for a faster journey morning and night and allowed me to stay in bed till seven o'clock. But this commuting meant that I had no university life and lived a purely academic existence outside the university system, missing all the debates and any kind of social life. I had to spend the whole day in the Psychology Department because, though I could work in the evenings at home, I didn't have the books there. I had to organize my day so that I could get the books when I needed them, plan what I was going to do in the evening, and go home equipped to do it. This put a bit of discipline in my very undisciplined life and redeemed my department's faith in the possibility of my obtaining a degree.

Chapter 6

The Irish aren't great singers, but they have great songs. One of my favorites is the Republican anti-Free State song:

> Take it down from the mast, Irish traitors,
> It's the flag we Republicans claim.
> It can never belong to Free Staters
> For you've brought on it nothing but shame.
> Leave it to those who are willing
> To uphold it in war and in peace,
> The men who intend to do killing
> Until England's tyranny cease.

Another one I like is "The Jolly Ploughboy," of which a gutless version has been made for popular Irish consumption. Its original words, banned not surprisingly in Southern Ireland, include:

> Some men fight for silver,
> Others fight for gold.
> But the IRA are fighting
> For the land De Valera sold.

About the time I was traveling every day between Cookstown and Belfast, I began to take into consideration the fact that all was not well in the South of Ireland. There was our Free State, our glorious tricolor, and the slums of Dublin and our people emigrating from the forgotten West. This thought tempered my mad Republican beliefs. I began looking at the Ireland I wanted to unite, and I realized that the task was not to free the Six Counties but to start all over again the national revolution. There were *no* free counties anywhere in Ireland. The Irish had replaced the British in twenty-six of the counties, but they had done nothing to change the system. Back in 1897, James Connolly, the only real socialist of the 1916 rebellion, had been saying, "Remove the British and raise the tricolor over Dublin Castle tomorrow, and Ireland's problems will remain, because Ireland's problems are economic and social." And it was still true. When I'd first gone back to Queen's after my mother's death, I couldn't concentrate on academic work and I'd spent my time, when I wasn't walking the streets of Belfast, reading anything I could lay my hands on so long as it had nothing to do with psychology. I'd read Frank O'Connor's life of Michael Collins, *The Big Fellow,* and this sparked off my disillusionment with Ireland. In the aftermath of 1916, when things were working up to the 1921 treaty in an atmosphere of sporadic violence and oppression, the different political tendencies in Ireland, represented by men like Collins, Arthur Griffith, and De Valera, had united with the attitude, "Let's get the British out first, and we'll sort out the problems later." But they fell apart too soon to carry out the second part of this program, and they fell apart, not on the basis of their political differences, but from personal jealousy. De Valera was smuggled out of Ireland ostensibly to raise support in

America for the Irish cause, while Collins and Griffith ran the government set up by the rebels under the noses of the English occupiers. Collins's prestige soared, and when De Valera came scurrying back, he was jealous of Collins. Collins, never noted for his tact, treated De Valera arrogantly, and between the pettiness of the two of them, they helped to ruin one of this century's finest revolutions. The patriots died. The politicians took over, and their shadow still looms large over Ireland today.

I see myself as something of a Collins. I don't view him as a hero: he was basically an aggressive, bullying type of person, almost a dictator. He had his place in the army, because he was a fighter with a good strategic brain, but he was totally undiplomatic, so arrogantly honest that he was annoying. He was the wrong person to send to England to negotiate the treaty with Lloyd George because he wasn't flexible at all, and he knew he shouldn't have gone, but being stubborn he went nonetheless. "Early this morning I signed my death warrant," he wrote to a friend on the day he signed the treaty. "I thought at the time how odd, how ridiculous— a bullet may just as well have done the job five years ago." * Earlier the English had put a price of £10,000 on Collins's head, but he walked freely through Dublin, avoiding all their traps, protected by the common people. Less than a year after the signing of the treaty, with the English gone from Ireland, he was mysteriously ambushed and shot on a road in his own county of Cork.

I feel a kindred spirit with the arrogant personality of Collins, and I believe that I'm in much the same situation as he. Basically I have no place in organized politics. By

* Frank O'Connor: *Death in Dublin*, New York, 1937. Originally titled *The Big Fellow*.

coming to the British Parliament, I've allowed the people to sacrifice me at the top and let go the more effective job I should be doing at the bottom.

Anyway, reading about the Collins–De Valera duel—which De Valera won, because he was a politician and politicians always win—I realized that in spite of all the emotion and the songs of glory, we ourselves were responsible for the failure to complete the revolution of 1916. I began moving away from traditional Republicanism to being generally opposed to the system. I didn't know what I was in favor of, but I knew I was against the system, which I hadn't yet learned enough jargon to term "capitalist." It was a subconscious journey to being a socialist, though I didn't call myself a socialist then. The problem in Northern Ireland, I decided, was not partition. If we took away partition, what did we join? If we had a truly free Ireland on the other side, we would have something to join, but what was the point of ending partition merely to alter the boundaries of injustice? At that stage I was saying to myself, "Okay, let's forget about partition; let's start working within the present framework. All right, so you don't want to be British. But you're British whether you like it or not. Let's go and ask for British democracy. If they're going to make us British by law, we must be British by standard of living as well." And over the months of 1968, I moved away from Republicanism to concern for nonpolitical social justice.

That summer I worked for my Uncle Tom Heaney in the pub. My grandmother had died, and the pub now belonged to him and to Barney. Tom was providing us with £5 a week, and so as not to be under an obligation to him, I worked it off, pulling pints. Compared with the average English pub, a pub in Northern Ireland is a dreary place.

If they only had dartboards on the wall, at least people might throw darts and not notice the general lack of excitement. People sit around talking about horses and women and women and horses, and the weather. And if anyone says anything about money, that's bad, for the conversation inevitably comes round to the cost of living and the whole question of the British subsidy to Northern Ireland, and before you know where you are, you are on the forbidden subject, politics. So I got quite bored, serving in the bar. Since I was there, the customers wouldn't talk about women, and with half their subject matter denied them, it was: horses, silence; horses, silence. To break the monotony, I'd try to get into conversation with anybody of reasonable intelligence, and possibly ask them where they worked. "In the new cement factory," they might say, and I would naturally ask some such question as "How many people do they employ there?" which led to "Who runs it? How are the employees selected?" But these were dangerous waters and I was a troublemaker for fishing in them. For the sake of a quiet life, you were supposed never to talk about the normal things that people talk about in any other place. However, underneath the conspiracy of silence, frustration was mounting. People like myself were getting sick, sore, and tired of being told, "In the interests of peace, say nothing." And this was, I believe, the roots of the civil-rights movement. At some point in a country's history there are enough people who feel the same way at the same time to create a force and change the pattern of events. That's what happened in Northern Ireland in the autumn of 1968.

The Civil Rights Association had been in existence for two years, during which time it had been doing ordinary constitutional things like writing to Members of Parliament, and getting nowhere by these methods. There was only one thing to do, they decided, and that was to take the movement to the people, so on August 24, 1968, they organized a civil-rights march from Coalisland to Dungannon, a distance of some three miles. I read about it in a newspaper and thought to myself, Civil-rights march! Excellent idea! It's about time somebody did something about the situation in Northern Ireland. And I set off to join it with my young brother and a friend.

At Coalisland there were masses of people milling around, selling civil-rights rosettes, eating oranges, and generally behaving as if they were at a carnival. The march was supposed to start at six o'clock on this bright August evening, but of course it started late, and it wasn't until about seven o'clock that we trudged off up the road led by a band of children playing accordions. We had been told this was a nonsectarian, nonpolitical march—for all that the demands we were making were political. Nevertheless politically minded young people had turned up with the banners of their associations—the Young Liberals, the Young Socialists, and so on— but they weren't allowed to carry them. The marchers were interspersed with various bands, playing "Who Fears to Speak of '98" and "Faith of Our Fathers." "Faith of Our Fathers" is a Catholic hymn which has been degraded by frequent playing at Nationalist gatherings and is one song I hate to hear at a political meeting, because it betrays the old mentality that equates Irish and Catholic. But we had a bash at "Faith of Our Fathers" anyway: so much for nonsectarian. We had stewards marshalling up who thought we were in the army, and kept singing out, "Pick up your feet! March in fours! One, two; one, two!" and everyone was just roaring at them. It was an event. It was the first civil-rights demonstration Northern Ireland had ever seen, and we all jogged along happily, eating oranges and smoking cigarettes, and people came out of their houses to join the fun. Marchers were dropping off at every pub on the way, and the whole thing had a sort of good-natured, holiday atmosphere, with the drunk men lolloping in and out of this supposedly serious demonstration.

Then we got to Dungannon, and the carnival feeling faltered. There was a police cordon across the road. We weren't going to be allowed into the town. At first the marchers only got half-heartedly annoyed, and some of them were roaring across on first-name terms to policemen they knew, but when the officer in charge came over and said that in the interests of the peace the march was being rerouted into the Catholic section of Dungannon, the whole atmosphere changed. Most of the people on the march hadn't really thought about civil rights: they had come, with a sort of friendly curiosity, to hear something. I do believe that then for the first time it dawned on people that Northern Ireland was a series of Catholic and Protestant ghettos. The meeting got very angry, though it was still a passive anger, with very little pushing and shoving of the police. Some men were calling out that we should force our way through, and the lines of the march were breaking formation and crowding up to the police. Everyone forgot about the accordion-playing children, about to be squashed between the opposing forces. Then my young brother grabbed a megaphone and bellowed through it: would the drunk men get out of the march, would the women take the children out of the march and get out of the way themselves. People made a move to do as he said until they realized the orders came from a fifteen-year-old boy, when they said, "My God, what's he talking about? You'd think there was going to be trouble." So John himself started leading the children to safety.

Meanwhile the leaders of the Civil Rights Association, which had called the march, were organizing a meeting there on the spot, in front of the police cordon. A lorry was brought up as a platform, and chairs and a microphone were put on the back of it, and the organizers announced that we weren't going to force our way into Dungannon because this was a nonviolent march. They were beginning to lose their hold on the marchers, though. People shouted, "What's the point of saying we'll get civil rights when you let them stop us having *this* civil right?" Gerry Fitt, the Republican Labour Member at Westminster for Belfast West, tried to match the feeling of the meeting, which was becoming more angry and rowdy by the minute. "If one of those black bastards of the Northern Ireland Gestapo puts a hand on any man here, I'll lead you through!" he stormed. Just at that moment a policeman with a big blackthorn stick struck a man, and the crowd literally cheered, dragged Gerry off the platform, and pushed him up to the front to keep his promise. Gerry fought his way back to the platform, scrambled up, and said, "Remember, there are women and children amongst us." Betty Sinclair, chairman and leading light of the Civil Rights Association in those days, got up, fearing the movement would be discredited if a fight broke out. "This is a nonpolitical, peaceful demonstration. Anyone who wants to fight should get out and join the IRA," she said. And the crowd roared back, "Where do we join?" Betty then realized that without any forethought at all she had organized a march in Coalisland, a town that was 90 per cent Republican; she had brought them out; they had been frustrated by the police;

and she had nothing constructive to offer them. She decided that the only thing she could safely do was wind up the meeting. "We'll end the meeting now, ladies and gentlemen," she said, "and before we go, we'll sing the civil-rights anthem." Nobody had heard of civil rights before, never mind the civil-rights anthem, so she went on, "The civil-rights anthem, 'We Shall Overcome.'" Like Sir Malcolm Sargent at the Promenade Concerts, she raised her arms and started, "We shall overcome . . . ," and everybody else started, "A nation once again . . ." By the time we'd got to the end of the first verse of our anthem, Betty and all her friends had scuttled into the lorry and driven off, leaving the population of Coalisland outside the town of Dungannon.

After that we sat down in big circles all over the road and sang rebel songs till midnight. There were one or two scuffles in Dungannon in which individuals who went into the town were beaten up by angry Unionists, but that was all. The police were very good-natured. They really didn't know what to do about us. It was a situation they'd never faced before, so they left us there to sing till we were tired, and then we all went home. It wasn't a fiasco precisely, that first march: at least it wakened people up a bit, but it seemed to have no echo in the weeks that followed and everybody was prepared to forget about it. I went back to the pub and thought about it and wondered when the next march would be held. I felt very cynical about the performance of the politicians and organizers: it was hilarious to see how out of touch they were with the people they supposedly represented. They thought they could come down, make big speeches, and be listened to respectfully, but when the people all got out together, they had turned round and said in effect to the politicians, "Clear off, you don't even *think* the way we think." And that's exactly what the politicians did: they cleared off.

In spite of their "civil-rights" label, the politicians had demanded *Catholic* equality and majority rule for *Catholic* areas. People like myself had not come to support such demands. We had come because we wanted to be involved— we were not quite sure in what. We knew something was wrong with a society where the rate of unemployment rarely fell below 10 per cent, where half the houses lacked at least one basic amenity. The politicians tried to tell us it was a nonpolitical demonstration; but though our politics were crude in those days, we were more politically aware than "the leaders" in that we refused to accept their logic that the problem could be seen in terms of Catholic versus Protestant.

Our system is one in which the basic divide is thought to be along religious lines, in which it is quite rational for a man to believe he is sentenced to unemployment for the crime of being a Catholic. But he is not. He is sentenced to unemployment because there are not enough jobs, and there are not enough jobs because investment is made on grounds of profit, not on grounds of people's needs. The crowd at that first-ever civil-rights march was interested in people's needs.

I also thought about the strength of feeling the march had shown, the amount of frustration people felt, and their readiness to release this frustration in wanton violence. But mainly I was just glad I'd seen people standing there outside Dungannon saying all the things they had never dared to say in the pub. People were coming into the pub now and saying quietly, "Were you on the march? Wasn't it great?"

So when the next march, to be held in Londonderry on

October 5, was announced, I welcomed it. Londonderry, traditionally called simply Derry, is the flash point of Northern Ireland. Because of the Siege of Londonderry in 1689—when the citizens inside the walls held out against the Catholic besiegers for 105 days before help came—it has enormous emotional value as a symbol to the Protestants, but it also has among the worst records in housing, employment, and political manipulation in the whole country. It is a place where passions don't need much to be aroused, and the Minister of Home Affairs, Mr. William Craig, banned the march. The reaction to the ban showed how far people's resignation had begun to crack. In the past when things were banned, you complained, you sulked, and you went home. More people turned up to the Derry march because it was banned than would have come if the government had done nothing about it. The silence was beginning to be broken.

I went to Derry on October 5 and found there an atmosphere that the city had never had before. Ordinarily Derry is a dead city: about one in five of the men is unemployed and the whole feeling of the place is depressed. But it was electric that day. You could see it on people's faces—excitement, or alarm, or anger. Derry was alive. My friends and I didn't know where the march was beginning, and we were afraid to ask, in case we asked the wrong person and got clobbered for our trouble. But we found it in the end and started off.

We hadn't got more than a couple of hundred yards up the street when we were stopped by masses of police. There were a few scuffles. The police took our banners away and knocked a few people over the head. Gerry Fitt had been injured and nobody knew what had happened to him. Once again the organizers decided to hold a meeting. There was no platform this time, but someone produced a chair, and Betty Sinclair got up on it, said her piece about its being a peaceful march, and suggested we should all go home. That was always her attitude: like the Grand Old Duke of York, lead the people up to the police, then lead them down again and send them home. It works the first time, and the second, and perhaps the third, but finally people say, "We didn't come here to go home," and all hell breaks loose. People were shouting, "If you don't want to get through, get out of the way!" and the mood was getting uglier. Here there was no carnival atmosphere and these weren't people who had come out for the fun of something new. These were men who had no work, these were the real men of no property. Their grievances were genuine, and the more the police stopped them from marching, the more bitter they became.

Then Eamonn McCann got up on the chair. This was the first time I'd seen him and he was a legendary figure to me. His escapades at Queen's had gone down in the university annals, and as a result of them he had been sent down. He was a weird mixture of irresponsibility and responsible, original, intelligent political thought. He put it to the marchers that they had three choices: they could go home, they could hold a meeting there, or they could walk into the police cordon until each successive row was beaten into the ground. "There's no point in standing here and screaming," he said. "Decide rationally what you're going to do, and organize to do it." The police knew that Eamonn was the real threat —he was turning a mob into a nonviolent force. So they charged.

I had been watching the police and I'd seen them filter down both sides of the march, so that now they encircled us. When we turned to go back down the street and re-form, we found we were trapped. There were policemen to the right and the left, to the fore and the aft, and they just moved in on all four sides, with truncheons and heels and boots, and beat everybody off the street. Then the water cannons came out and hosed the streets. Quite deliberately they hosed in upstairs windows and shop fronts, and they went right across Craigavon Bridge, hosing all the onlookers. The police just went mad.

Derry was on every newspaper in Ireland, every newspaper in Britain. It was being flashed on every television screen in the world. Telefis Eireann (the Southern Ireland television network) had a smart cameraman who filmed the whole thing, sold the film to every company who could get their hands on it, and gave Harold Wilson a private showing. And Ireland was up in arms: you can slowly crush the Irish, you can take the ground from under their feet and they won't notice they're sinking down; but if you hit them, they will hit back. So the Unionist government did the civil-rights movement a favor. They gave it life in one day. Without the police, it would have taken much longer to get off the ground.

While everyone was running madly around me, I was standing still—not because I hadn't panicked, but because panic had a different effect on me. I was standing almost paralyzed, watching the expressions on the faces of the police. Arms and legs were flying everywhere, but what horrified me was the evil delight the police were showing as they beat people down, then beat them again to prevent them from getting up, then trailed them up and threw them on for somebody else to give them a thrashing. It was as though they had been waiting to do it for fifty years. Perhaps because I was the only person who wasn't running, I wasn't touched at all, but as I was standing there a young fellow came up, grabbed me by the arm, and said, "For Christ's sake, move!" Just as he pushed me in front of him, which left him standing where I had been, a policeman clobbered him, splitting his head down the side. Even though the blood was pouring down his face, the police weren't prepared to leave him alone: they made him run the gauntlet, until we got him out beyond the cordon and took him into a barber's shop. When he was roughly patched up, we brought him to Altnagelvin Hospital for stitches, and later when we went back to collect him, we were asked, "Was he one of those people at the demonstration?"

"We don't really know," I said. "He was hit by something, anyway, and brought in here to get stitched."

"Well, if he was one of those demonstrators, he didn't get hit hard enough." Such was the impartial attitude of those ministering to the sick. They wouldn't tell us who he was, where he was, or how he was, and having discovered the color of the skin of Altnagelvin Hospital, we decided the sooner we got out of there the better.

After that I walked into a pub, literally shaking, and swallowed one double whiskey neat without tasting it. So began my civil-rights commitment and my whiskey drinking.

Chapter 7

For three days I hardly ate a bite, I was so sick with indignation and horror. If I could, I would have gone to every police barracks in Northern Ireland and systematically slaughtered the inmates. But common sense in the end prevailed, and in arguments with my friends, I worked out a saner attitude: a few of them thought that the only way to deal with the tactics we'd seen the police use in Derry was to arm and wage war against them. I came to believe, by thinking about the futility of the violence we had seen, that we needed more than anything else to build up a disciplined, nonviolent force. If we hadn't panicked and run in Derry, the police couldn't have done the amount of damage they did.

The history-making Derry march was on Saturday, October 5, 1968. The following Tuesday, the eighth, Queen's University reopened for the new academic year, which should have been my final year. I went up to Belfast thinking I had changed, and I found that everybody had. The atmosphere at Queen's was joltingly different. The silence barrier was down. Derry was being talked about in the lecture rooms, in the tutorial rooms, in the snackbar at dinner, in the cloak-rooms, in the showers, in the bar. No matter where you went, there was serious discussion going on: who organized the march?; who was to blame for what happened?; where had things gone wrong? People were talking and thinking about the society they were living in—not as an intellectual exercise, but realistically and emotionally and as if it mattered. Most people were angry and indignant, but we also noticed for the first time that the 5 per cent intellectual cream of the country that had got to Queen's had its extreme right-wing element, for there were students saying, "They didn't get enough. It's a pity the police didn't kill half a dozen of them."

The year before, a Joint-Action Committee had been formed by representatives from the different political organizations who got together to arrange a demonstration against the banning of Republican Clubs. These people found each other again, resurrected the committee, and announced there was to be a march to Belfast's City Hall the next day, the ninth, in protest against the police brutality in Derry. Once before I'd been involved in a demonstration, when we were asked to show solidarity with the foreign students at Queen's, whose fees had been raised by 125 per cent by the government. On that occasion we couldn't get fifty students on the streets to complain. But on October 9, two thousand turned up spontaneously. All the old complacent attitudes were gone.

In Northern Ireland, if you plan a march, you must file for it—you must give details of time, route, and so forth to the police, and someone must sign to take responsibility as organizer. This was done and all two thousand of us set off from the university on our announced route to the City Hall. It let us into Shaftesbury Square, the students' shopping area, but before we got there, on home ground as it were, we were brought up short by the police. There were fifty counter-demonstrators ahead, determined to defend the loyal Unionist territory of Shaftesbury Square from what they saw as a papist invasion inspired by the IRA. The police wouldn't allow a confrontation, we must get to the City Hall another way. Obediently we took another road, which made the march a bit longer and brought us out at the back, instead of the front, of the City Hall. The "loyalists" had got there before us and so had the police. We were told we must wait to come round to the front until the opposition had been cleared, so we sat down in the road to wait. And we waited, and we waited. Some three hours later, the police still hadn't managed to shift the fifty "loyalists," and the demonstration broke up. It might have seemed a failure, but our behavior that day earned us a great deal of respect in the community. The demonstration was well organized, well disciplined, and it had its touch of humanity. Our organizer, Fred Taggart, later to become president of the Students' Union, was so frustrated by the continual stalling of the police that he ended up just standing in the middle of Linen Hall Street crying. And of course the *Daily Mirror* never misses anything. Next day there was Fred on the front of the *Mirror* with great big tears dripping off the end of his chin. We had behaved responsibly, we had been badly treated by the police, and poor Fred Taggart was reduced to tears. The general public was a hundred per cent with the students—something pretty new in student demonstrations.

People's Democracy was born, though not named, that night at a discussion which lasted till one o'clock next morning. We got back from our failed march and went straight into session in the university debating hall, realizing what frustration the ordinary man must feel, having something much more fundamental than a protest march denied him every day of his life.

We decided we would work for six aims: one man, one vote; a fair drawing of electoral boundaries; freedom of speech and assembly; repeal of the Special Powers Act (which gives the police almost unlimited power of arrest and detention); and a fair allocation of jobs and houses. All these aims, which emerged from that student discussion, were to be endorsed later by the civil-rights movement as a whole. But the students, as they developed, came to realize that to demand merely a fair allocation of existing resources was on its own futile: it was merely asking for an equal share of Northern Ireland's poverty. The basic problem was a shortage of jobs and houses: the basic answer to supply the insufficiency.

During that impassioned debate, the political personalities of Queen's naturally enough aired their views, but for the first time the ordinary students found they had a voice and a point of view, and because of this the politicos agreed not to impose their leadership on the new student body. No one wanted the overtones they would give it; we didn't want time and energy wasted in ideological quarrels; and we did want unpolitical, uncommitted students to put their weight behind the civil-rights cause. So from the ordinary people in the hall, ten without political affiliation were elected to what became known as the "Faceless Committee." I was one of the ten.

The Faceless Committee turned out to be not very aptly named. For a start we all had the kind of face you don't forget. Most of the men were bearded. Kevin Boyle, a lecturer in the Law Faculty, had a kind of Trotsky beard; Fergus

Woods was a dark, cuddly, beardy fellow; Ian Goodall had a ginger beard and long hair; Malcolm Miles had dark, sinister eyes and a Chinese mustache-beard. The Faceless Committee were, in fact, the weirdest-looking bunch of people you ever saw. The other three men were two short-back-and-sides exceptions, Joe Martin and Eddie McCamely, and Michael ("Kick the fuzz") O'Kane, and there were three girls on it, Anne McBurney, Patricia Drinan, and myself. We went into session immediately the meeting ended at one o'clock to draft a leaflet, and hauled our artist, Drew Plunkett, out of bed to design a poster. The poster he designed, a gaunt, outstretched hand, with "March for your rights" written down the side of it, was both the voting hand and a sort of parody of the Red Hand of Ulster, the emblem on the Ulster flag. It was to become very popular. The next evening our leaflet and poster were approved by a mass meeting of the students, and taken off to be printed. John D. Murphy, our printer, got the material late at night, and only then noticed that our organization had no name. To comply with the law, he had to put the name of the organization responsible at the bottom of the leaflet, and, the story goes, he read through it, decided it was all about people's rights, and christened us People's Democracy. No one has ever been prepared to claim sole credit for our christening. The name anyway emerged, and it stuck.

Our next march was to be October 16, and I volunteered to sign for it: most people had their parents to worry about, but I was more or less my own master and had nothing to lose. Off we trotted again, and this time, in spite of a reroute, we got to the City Hall and held a very orderly, constructive meeting. There was none of the "Smash the bourgeoisie" type of rhetoric that you usually get at student meetings. We spoke about ordinary, simple issues, like jobs, houses, and involvement in the system, because we were talking to people to whom these were the issues that mattered. The police didn't interfere, on the principle that if we held our meeting, we would lose interest in the whole thing, go away contentedly and never trouble them again.

After that we decided we weren't just a marching machine. That meeting had established some form of contact with the Belfast people, and we thought it would be a good idea to spread this by going into the provinces of Ulster and setting up local organizations. Marching was a good way of drawing attention to what we were protesting about, but we wanted more—we wanted the oppressed people to become involved in making the decisions which affected their own lives. After all, they were the only ones who in the end could solve their problems. We also hoped that at a local level people would see their problems were problems of class, not religion.

Newry was the first town to have an organization of its own. A dozen or so People's Democracy members went to Newry one morning, distributed leaflets throughout the town, held an open-air meeting—like the apostles preaching the gospel—in the afternoon, then called an indoor meeting for the evening. At this meeting, the local people set up their own civil-rights organization, and began considering how to tackle their local grievances. A week later People's Democracy sent apostles simultaneously to Dungannon and Omagh; and they ran into trouble. The Paisleyites were waiting for them.

The Reverend Ian Paisley, self-styled Moderator of the Free Presbyterian Church of Ulster, is to my mind a dangerous man and an influence for evil. When the Protestant working class realize—as I believe they're beginning to do—that the ruling Unionist Party doesn't serve their interests, their normal reaction will be to move left, either into the Northern Ireland Labour Party or to become the most militant socialists of the lot of us. Paisley's aim is to secure this Protestant working-class support for himself, thus preventing it from moving left. For the Reverend Ian Paisley does not hate Catholics as he appears to do: what he hates are socialists.

He came to power in the 1950's preaching a militant anti-popery, and his appeal for his followers lies both in their strong religious feelings and in their fear that the depressed Catholic third of the population would, by getting a share of power, rob them of the small measure of prosperity and security they now have. Paisley fools them into thinking that their strength *as* the working class lies in beating down the Catholics, and as long as he can keep them away from—and in fact turn them against—the Catholic working class, he need never fear the unity of the proletariat. His influence reaches over the Protestant defenders of the Northern Ireland system to the working-class Catholics who, deprived of the support of their fellow workers, seek strength in an all-class Catholic alliance. Thus they fall into the same trap as the Protestants. Discrimination against Catholics within the system helps widen the division in the working class, and has effectively been used by the Orange Order-manipulated leaders of the state. The tragedy of the situation is that by aligning themselves with those who work against their interests but share their religion, the working class of my country, Protestant and Catholic, perpetuates its own misery.

Paisley's big appeal is to the Protestant poor, but he is also supported by wealthy Unionists who want to keep Protestant and Catholic apart for their own ends, and by the real bigots who *do* hate Catholicism. But it seems clear to me that Paisley's hatred is not of the Catholic Church: his hatred is of everything on the left, and his love is his own power.

The Paisleyites are sort of caricatures of Ulster Protestants, out-Britishing the British by a long shot. They are mad keen on the Union Jack, but the interesting question to put to them is: How about Harold Wilson, our British socialist Prime Minister?, and they'll swear blind that Harold Wilson isn't British. Only the Tories are British, and the further they move from fascism, the more they are declining from British standards. The Paisleyites don't really want to have anything to do with England, because England has forgotten it's British. At one point they were talking about UDI—a Unilateral Declaration of Independence, on the model of Ian Smith and Rhodesia—which would leave Ulster the only unsullied little corner of all the British Isles. But so far they've not been strong enough to pull it off. Such is the delusion and confusion of a people deprived of their economic rights. They know something is wrong, but they don't know how to put it right. Because of their fears of the Catholics, created and continually strengthened by the demagogues and power-mongers at the top, they seek refuge in the past, and in the full realization of the promise of Lord Carson: a Protestant state for a Protestant people. What they've got, after fifty years of Unionism, is a Protestant state for the Protestant rich.

Paisley's forays to the Vatican and the World Council of Churches and so on, to denounce the Pope, have made him seem something of a buffoon, but on his home ground we must take him seriously. As well as a small chain of Free Presbyterian churches over the country, he has a political force and many of his supporters are members of the heavily

armed B Specials, for whose retention he has constantly campaigned; or of the Ulster Volunteer Force, a civilian part-time
army whose strength is unknown. He heads or is supported by
a variety of organizations whose purposes are obscure and
whose titles arresting, like the Purple Sons of Tubal-cain.

After People's Democracy's visit to Newry, the Paisleyites
evidently decided that this looked like a successful tactic and
would have to be stopped. They broke up our meetings at
Dungannon and Omagh. At Dungannon, the PD party
managed to escape from the open-air meeting into a restaurant, but the pursuing Paisleyites broke down the door,
walked over the manager's wife, and wrecked the place. The
people in Omagh had their car almost overturned and their
loudspeaker equipment smashed. They got a seventy-miles-
an-hour police escort out of town in case they were ambushed, but in neither place did the police do more than the
minimum—quite naturally: it suited their purposes to look
as if they were doing their duty, but make sure we were
ineffective in the future by having no equipment. We then
tried a few meetings in Belfast. The same thing happened,
we weren't even allowed to begin. So we weren't getting the
education across, but we *were* leaving a trail of violence
behind us. Until we thought of a better tactic for communi-
cating, we called a halt to these useless meetings and stuck
mainly to mass leafleting. There was a plan to produce a PD
newspaper but it collapsed for lack of finance.

Meanwhile, back at Queen's, our movement was turning
into an experiment in mass democracy. We had been a society
of dead ducks before, but events were showing that enthusiasm and concern had been lying dormant in every one of us.
Meetings were held most nights of the week on university
premises. At first, because we weren't a recognized student

society, there was some trouble about giving us rooms to hold our meetings in; but our argument was that since most of us were students, no one could prevent us from sitting down where we liked and talking. Or we would ask another society to open a debate and, after half an hour, adjourn it and hand it over to us. At each meeting a new chairman was elected—just somebody from the body of the hall—and his sole function was to control the order of speaking. When the chairman was in place, we'd decide on the agenda. People stuck their hands up: "Can we have such-and-such on the agenda?" and down it all went, and we'd vote on the order of importance. Fair enough, this wasted twenty minutes of the meeting, but at least it meant that everybody agreed on what we were doing and we didn't spend hours wrangling about doing something else.

Anyone who wanted could come to the meeting, and sometimes Paisleyites came to tell us we were all Fenian scum. We listened calmly to them, then one of us would get up and explain why we weren't, as it happened, Fenian scum, and that the Paisleyites had the wrong idea entirely. All this reasonableness and tolerance put them off trying to break up meetings. It was more or less impossible to create havoc in a PD meeting: everybody was prepared to let you stand up and rant and rave till you were exhausted; if you heckled from the audience, you were asked to wait a few moments and then you would be allowed to speak; if you continued heckling, the speaker gave way and handed you the microphone, and there you were, stuck with it, and some seven hundred politely interested faces watching you.

Decisions were taken by majority vote, and handed over to the Faceless Committee to be put into effect. And the work got done. Someone on the committee would say, "Look, we've got fifty letters to answer," so we went out and got five people who answered ten each, and we didn't need a secretary. The Civil Rights Association couldn't understand how we could operate without officers, and they disapproved of the majority-vote decisions. "What happens," they said, "if you find yourself saddled with a majority vote to be violent?" Our argument was that people determined on violence wouldn't be persuaded out of it by a chairman and a treasurer; if everybody in PD was thirsting for blood, at least we'd know about it, and those who personally disapproved could steer clear. In fact, because we discussed things rationally, there was less violence on marches organized by us than on other marches.

People's Democracy never ended. The mass meeting began at half past seven in the evening, and when it was over people broke up into their own friendship circles, to continue the discussions in private flats. Or we went on to Smokey's, the university café, and when that closed down, to the Hobbit, the late-night café, where the revolution continued into the small hours. The Hobbit had never been so prosperous. People hadn't previously bothered with this open-to-half-two-in-the-morning, baked-potato lark, because everybody went to bed early in Belfast: at midnight we all turned into pumpkins. Now the revolution had begun and the Hobbit was thriving.

We began to find we had enemies on the staff, but also friends. Every time we had a demonstration and one of us was caught by the police, he was up before the Vice-Chancellor: "You'd better behave!" The Vice-Chancellor himself was prepared to turn a blind eye on our activities, rather than provoke a worse student backlash, but attitudes generally were hardening, and some of us were kept inside the university only because members of staff fought for us tooth and nail. However, we went on gaining strength and becoming more and more a body to be reckoned with.

On United Nations Day, October 24, we decided to demonstrate in Stormont, the Northern Ireland Parliament building. Since it was United Nations Day in Human Rights year, Gerry Fitt—a member of both the Stormont and Westminster Parliaments—was to ask for a suspension of Standing Orders so that a Human Rights Bill, sponsored by a Liberal MP, Miss Sheelagh Murnaghan, could be discussed. Seventy-two of us packed the public gallery. We used often to go to Stormont, and just peer over the gallery at ministers we disapproved of until they blushed. That day, Gerry wasn't given leave to discuss human rights: rather than consider the bill, they adjourned the House, and Gerry walked out in protest, followed by one or two other Opposition members. Before the rest of the members could get out, we filed unobtrusively out of the public gallery, down the stairs, to the central lobby, where we sat down. Now here, in Stormont, the police had no right to intervene: the only person who could have us thrown out was the Speaker, and the Speaker hesitated to do it. We said we weren't leaving until the MP's read and signed a statement saying they were in favor of introducing the Human Rights Bill, and because they had failed to discuss it in Parliament, we decided to discuss it ourselves.

This was where I came to some sort of prominence in PD, for I chaired that debate. We were there from three o'clock in the afternoon to about seven o'clock, and we could be heard all over the Houses of Parliament. Every time we spotted an MP, we called him down to sign our statement, and honorable Members of Parliament were hiding behind pillars and peeping out to see what was going on. As well as the seventy-two students inside the building, who were covering the floor of the central lobby with civil-rights stickers, there were a further couple of hundred students outside, preventing the MP's from getting out by any of the doors. The only door we left unguarded was the service door at the back, so that the Members had to suffer the indignity of sneaking out through the kitchens, if they wanted to avoid us.

I was sent to ferret out William Craig, Minister of Home Affairs, and as such responsible for the police, to ask him to come and give us an account of his stewardship. This proved a lively task: I had to make a quick dive up one set of stairs, past two policemen, only to meet three more at the top who promptly escorted me back to ground level. As soon as I got down, the tactic was to make a dart at the other staircase, pound up it, get to the top, and again be brought down by the forces of the law—much to everybody's amusement. Craig was not to be got, but they sent us Captain Long, the Minister of Education. Basically we were quite fond of Captain Long. He was always sent to speak to us, however inappropriate the occasion, not because he was Minister of Education, but because, being placid, he was the only member of the government who could be trusted not to lose his temper. When he came down, Fergus Woods, the comedian of the PD, stood up and said, "Every boy scouts' troop has a poor little fellow who is always made to carry the water. Captain Long is the Unionist Party's water-carrying boy scout, and as such I would like to welcome him to our gathering." From then on, that was Captain Long's nickname among us. He gave us a little speech about the rugby match that had been played the day before, and we thanked him very much, said we were glad he enjoyed rugby, but wondered if he oughtn't to vacate his seat in Parliament for someone less interested in sport and more interested in governing.

On November 4, there was to be another march through Shaftesbury Square, and this time we told the police that there would be no rerouting. Since this was home territory, we felt we had the right to walk through it. We would go as far as we could, and if we were stopped, there would be no violence from us. By this time we had established our trust-worthiness with the police, although we had learned not to trust them, and when the march reached University Road, there was only a small police cordon. We stopped some twenty-five yards away from the cordon, while the first five of the Faceless Committee went up to the police to argue our case and ask permission to go through. The idea was that, if the first five were arrested, or beaten up and thrown into the police tenders, the next five would take their place, and the march would keep going forward in disciplined fives, forcing the police to attack five individuals time and time again.

When the first five reached the cordon, the police officers broke their line to gather round and argue with us—there were Paisleyites massing up the road, and they weren't going to permit a confrontation. And because the cordon had broken up, the rows of marchers behind us started splitting quietly and leaking round the edges of the cordon to the other side. Half a dozen rows had got round before the police noticed that the civil-rights banner was behind them. They then gave the alarm. Policemen, who had been hiding round corners in trucks, poured out of everywhere. They linked arms and started a sort of Nazi stomp up the road, throwing out their feet and kicking us as they went. We felt this was totally unwarranted: all they had to do was re-form the cordon and we would have stopped. But they didn't wait to find out, they just came charging on in a slow plod, and the marchers who had got beyond the cordon got caught up and bumped about. Meanwhile the Paisleyites were coming up behind the police in military formation, and for all that they hadn't filed for a march, there were no policemen keeping them in order.

Faced with the police charge, the students' immediate reaction was to sit down. I had the megaphone and I shouted through it: "Everybody sit down as quickly as possible, and then we'll see who's causing the violence!" and instead of running, everybody just flopped to the ground. The police hadn't time to stop marching: they stumbled over the first rows, and it didn't improve their tempers to know that television photographers were filming the Royal Ulster Constabulary falling over students in their eager stomp forward in the interests of peace. Finally the District Inspector (known from his PR visits to the university as "Everybody's Friend D.I. Bradley") established some sort of order among his forces, got them all up on their feet again, and formed the cordon. Finding the whole thing hilarious, I turned round to one of the policemen in the cordon and said, "There you are, you see! We're all sitting down comfortably!" I expected some kind of friendly-sarcastic answer, but this fellow immediately threw his foot out in a most violent kick which landed on my ankle, and knocked the feet from under me. "All but you, stupid bitch!" he said. And I found myself sitting very uncomfortably and very suddenly. Bernadette Devlin, poor creature, everybody's kid sister—immediately about twenty males were up and making for the constable, and I had to hobble up and get them to sit down again before the situation got out of control. We were a very self-disciplined lot: instead of giving the man a bashing, the students who had seen the incident began writing out reports of it, and getting other witnesses to sign. We'd been trained to do this by friends in the Society of Labour Lawyers. We knew more about legal evidence than the police did, we had more self-control, and we were better-humored: whichever way they took us, we always had the upper hand.

We knew that according to the law we could refuse to give a policeman any information, unless he arrested us; and we also knew that if we challenged a policeman for his name or number, he was obliged to tell us one of them. I turned to the constable who had kicked me and asked him his name. He refused to answer. He didn't meet my eyes, but looked straight ahead and kept his mouth shut. I asked the policeman beside him. "I don't know," said he, "I've never seen him before."

"Does he come from Belfast?"

"I don't know. I'm not from Belfast." This was a damaging admission: it meant that riot-squad policemen had been brought in from the countryside to deal with the nonviolent students. We had all this immediately written down, witnessed, and signed by the people who had heard it. Then I called the District Inspector over and said, "This man refuses to give me his name," and Mr. Bradley knew enough of the law to oblige the man to give it. He was a constable from Queen Street Barracks, Belfast. The D.I. wouldn't let me have his number, so I said, "Fair enough, I'll take my statement to the Queen Street Barracks and see what can be done about this disgusting behavior, lowering the tone of our force." We liked to make fun of them like that: they were the police who beat us, but when they behaved in an ignorant fashion we pulled them up for disgracing Northern Ireland. They couldn't win.

Later, when I went to the barracks, I found that this constable had apparently made a practice of kicking demonstrators and was so stupid he always got caught. My complaint, coming on top of several others, would be the last straw: out of the force he would go. And such was the extent of my political development at the time that ignorant thug though he was, I couldn't see the point of adding to Northern Ireland's unemployed. I took my statement home again, and until such time as he kicked somebody else, he probably remained in the police force.

On November 22, the government announced its proposals for "reform": the system of allocating publicly owned housing was to be changed, and local authorities were asked to submit schemes for doing it; there was to be a comprehensive reform and modernization of local government elections by the end of 1971; an official was to be appointed to look into citizens' grievances; a government-appointed commission was to take over the running of Derry from the local council.

To begin with, these were not reforms, but suggestions for reform. There was no commitment to the principle of one man, one vote. Nor was there any promise to deal with the basic problems of unemployment and bad housing. And the Special Powers Act remained on the Statute Book.

On the rest of Britain, the existence of the Special Powers Act in Northern Ireland only has the effect of preventing the United Kingdom from signing international conventions on human rights. But in Northern Ireland it means you can be arrested without a warrant and imprisoned without charge, denied recourse to habeas corpus, legal advice, or trial by jury; theoretically you could be held incommunicado for years; it means the police can enter and search a house without a warrant, declare curfews, prohibit meetings, deny the right to hold an inquest on someone who has died in custody. Among its many provisions is one blanket one, providing for the arrest of people who do anything "calculated to be prejudicial to the preservation of peace or maintenance of order in Northern Ireland and not specifically provided for in the regulations." So total is the power it gives the police and the Minister of Home Affairs that a leading member of the South African government has said he'd be prepared to swap all his repressive legislation for one Special Powers Act.

So, with nothing more than half-promises that all would yet be well, and with this noxious Act still on our backs, we—the students—didn't feel anything had been achieved: we felt we'd been sold down the river. The next event was Captain O'Neill's appeal to the nation, which was hilarious.

Captain Terence O'Neill, Prime Minister of Northern Ireland from 1963 until events forced him to resign in the spring of 1969, is a well-bred, middle-class English country gentleman. He knows it's bad form to discriminate, just as it's bad form to tuck your table napkin under your chin instead of putting it on your lap. He knows all the polite forms, but he carries them out mechanically. There is never any kind of spontaneity about anything he has to do. With this lack of warmth, and with his Eton-and-guards-regiment background, his main problem as Prime Minister of Northern Ireland was that at no stage did he ever belong. In the end he fell from power because he hesitated. He realized that Ulster had to go forward, and he wanted to bring it forward without losing anything, which was impossible. If there was to be any kind of progress, something in the tight Unionist structure had to give. If he had been a good politician, he could have widened democracy in Northern Ireland by widening the Unionist Party. But all he did was make liberal noises that didn't convince the Catholics while they did frighten the Protestant Unionist faction into thinking they were losing something. When he didn't follow his words with actions, the Protestant Unionist faction came to believe that if they protested loudly enough, there never would be any action. However, he kept on saying liberal things, and he would have to go. Meanwhile the civil-rights movement and the Catholic population got more and more frustrated waiting for a liberal tomorrow that never came. In any case, as far as we were concerned, he was essentially a Tory, growing rich on the low-wage, high-unemployment system that kept Northern Ireland in slavery.

Captain O'Neill decided to speak to the nation early in December 1968, and he must have sat at home for ages studying Churchill's speeches to get the right emotive intonation. "What kind of Ulster do you want?" he asked us. "I will accept whatever your verdict may be. If it is your decision that we should live up to the words 'Ulster is British,' which is part of our creed, then my services will be at your disposal to do what I can. But if you should want a separate, inward-looking, selfish and divided Ulster, then you must seek for others to lead you along the road, for I cannot and will not do it . . ." This was the prime minister of a country, reciting "The boy stood on the burning deck" for a political speech! The Minister of Home Affairs, William Craig, had been talking about Ulster being separate from Britain (he was sacked from the government by O'Neill on December 11, the day after the speech), and Captain O'Neill asked how could Ulster be separate without an army or navy of its own. The way it came across was, "For Christ's sake, somebody tell me where the army is and I'll declare UDI too," and this complete misinterpretation of what the poor man was trying to say left the students with no respect for Terence O'Neill.

But all over Northern Ireland, people were clustered round their television screens, dabbing their eyes as you do at an oversentimental film, and saying, "Poor fellow!" He ended his appeal by saying, "Support me! Show me you support me by any means you can!" and the next day the country went mad supporting O'Neill. Letters of sympathy started rolling in. "Dear Terence, Don't worry, we support you. Signed, Middle-aged woman." For almost a week, the middle page of the *Newsletter* was devoted to a list of names of people who supported O'Neill. The *Belfast Telegraph* printed a coupon that you cut out, filled in, and sent back, if you supported O'Neill—it was big bargain week: two pounds of butter for the price of one. "The man needs time," the civil-rights people said, backing down from any semblance of pressure. "We will give Captain Terence O'Neill time." And he hadn't offered them a solitary thing.

In reaction to the television speech, the various civil-rights bodies agreed to call a truce over Christmas. It was like Vietnam: a twenty-four-hour truce was declared in Vietnam, and a four-week truce in Northern Ireland. We like to take our time about these things. So we had a four weeks' turkey-eating session, while nothing changed in Northern Ireland. The students called no truce. We did cancel a march that was to have been held in Belfast on December 14, because we hadn't time to persuade people of the hollowness of Captain O'Neill's appeal, and in the pro-Captain Terence frenzy of the moment, a march would have seemed a useless provocation. And we agreed to alter the date of the Long March we were planning to make between Belfast and Derry. Originally this was timed to arrive in Derry on Christmas Day, but in view of the Prime Minister's speech and its effect on the country, we decided to put the start off till January 1, 1969. This would show the civil-rights movement was no temporary thing: the fight was going on into the New Year.

Chapter 8

Between October 5 and the end of 1968, People's Democracy, and I along with it, moved gradually and inexorably left. We had started off without any political affiliation, with very little political awareness even; the majority attitude then could be summed up as a sort of liberal belief in the necessity for justice. And, of course, we were pretty inexperienced. The more demonstrations we organized, the more we became convinced of the usefulness of the nonviolent method: it baffled the police, it baffled the Paisleyites, and it gave us each time a further lesson in self-discipline, which prepared us for the next stage. If we hadn't learned those lessons in the weeks from October to December, we wouldn't have survived the Long March to Derry.

The move leftwards had begun by the end of October, and it was due to the simple fact that the most effective solutions to the problems we discussed always turned out to be the solutions offered by the left. We educated ourselves into socialism. Night after night we sat down to four-hour-long meetings to discuss every aspect of every Northern Ireland problem: why we couldn't get through to the Protestant working class; what we should do to try to get through to them; why, when we made reasonable demands and stuck to our guns about getting them, some of our friends should turn round and call us mindless militants; how we could enlist responsible support and not remain a student-oriented student organization looking inward on student society. It was quite noticeable that at every PD meeting, more people were drifting left, not on an emotional basis, but on the basis of the discussions we had and the problems we faced.

A big contribution to our political education was made by the Young Socialists' Alliance, a group of young people of whom Michael Farrell was the most important. The Young Socialists had no definite theoretical formation—they were just young lefties, basic Marxists. One or two were obviously Stalinist, one or two obviously Trotskyist, and one or two were socialist by a kind of basic instinctive principle, without being sure what their theory of socialism was. I had a lot of sympathy with this last section, but I wasn't prepared to join the Young Socialists because of a kind of pettiness about them. Michael Farrell was the leader, a very clever young man who teaches liberal studies in the Belfast College of Technology. He had been a Catholic and at one time was studying for the priesthood, and had then gone through a process starting at extreme left-wing doctrinaire socialism, and ending up at original political exploration. He and Eamonn McCann of Derry are the two people who are doing the thinking of the left in Northern Ireland and who will in the end create its political philosophy. Michael had, from October onwards, a tremendous impact on the PD, by his consistent explanations of the best method of attacking the evils of society.

Second-in-command of the Belfast left was Cyril Toman.

Cyril was a theoretician: he preached the gospel according to St. Marx. He would take it out of his pocket at meetings and quote it in great big theoretical chunks of socialist jargon. He started every speech with: "This reminds me of the Sorbonne . . . ," and we got bored with this grand drawing of comparisons and roared back, "Never mind the Sorbonne! We're interested in the slums of Belfast." Cyril has always read all the books: I'm very fond of him as a person, but as a politician and a revolutionary, he ought to leave the books behind, because it's like somebody trying to cook a banquet for fifty people and carry the recipe book round with him as he goes. Cyril greatly resented the fact that he was number two instead of number one in the Young Socialists, and this put me off them. If they really believed in socialism, what did it matter whether you were number one or number fifty-one? However, in spite of ignoble power struggles, the Young Socialists were effective because they were more consistent than anybody else about what Northern Ireland needed, and because they were prepared to do the donkey-work. Others of us who were also consistent and did the slogging—painting the posters, sitting up all night to work out leaflets—found ourselves in a kind of nonpolitical sympathy with them.

By January, we were more and more moving to the left, but still we were at the stage where if the move became overt in any way, it frightened people off. We still had the attitude, "My God, we might be socialists!" and we scurried back to the middle. But this was decreasing slightly and for the activists, the Long March ended it. Everybody who stuck with the march the whole way—a perilous journey through Indian territory—came out of it conscious of a solidarity, a need to stick together, to share everything, work together and trust each other; and realizing we had one thing in common: we were socialists, and we believed socialism was worth struggling for. "Look," we said, "what's so frightening about being left—if it's the only way to get justice?"

The next stage of the development was: socialism in what context? If the Unionist Party system were ever broken there had to be something to put in its place, so that society could survive and the justice we were demanding become a reality. We knew there was no point in talking about socialism within the United Kingdom, for with a pseudo-socialist state in England, real socialism couldn't survive in a British Northern Ireland. It couldn't, in fact, survive without a national Irish movement. For me, the wheel was coming full circle; but with variations. I had moved from traditional, mad, emotional Republicanism to socialism in the context of Ulster; now I was joining my new-found socialism to my old belief in a united Ireland. Only in a thirty-two-county Ireland could socialism even begin to work. But I had realized that the essential problem was not to unite the country, but to unite the people, and this could only be done on the basis of socialism. At one stage in this development I was almost disowned by some of my Republican friends, who saw me as abandoning the cause; but by the time I'd completed the circle, events had changed them too, and even if they weren't as left as I was, they were prepared to respect my beliefs.

We had started in October as students involved in the whole of society, and to begin with we had a very responsible, quiet, well-disciplined image. But as the public relations work of Terence O'Neill—the only job he really did well—began to affect public opinion, we came to be considered militants. The respectable people in the Civil Rights Association didn't want to look militant and were on the wane. When we said we were marching, in spite of the Christmas truce, we were on the point of being discredited in the eyes of the various bodies in the civil-rights movement. Our only hope was that we would get through to the ordinary people, who hadn't believed in Terence O'Neill's speech, but who didn't see what they could do about it. Our function in marching from Belfast to Derry was to break the truce, to relaunch the civil-rights movement as a mass movement, and to show people that O'Neill was, in fact, offering them nothing. We knew we wouldn't finish the march without getting molested, and we were accused of going out looking for trouble. What we really wanted to do was pull the carpet off the floor to show the dirt that was under it, so that we could sweep it up; and to show the uselessness of the tactics of both the Unionist Party, who were stretching the carpet to prevent the dirt coming out; and of the civil-rights campaigners, who were tidying rou the edges of the carpet and forgetting about the real problems underneath.

But there was a little local difficulty in PD before all this became clear. It was decided to postpone the march from its original date before Christmas to an "indefinite date." This was taken by moderates in PD to mean, in effect, cancellation. Then the Young Socialists said they were marching from January 1 to 4, whether anyone else did or not, and the question came up at a meeting held during the Christmas vacation. This raised queries about the structure of our movement: when was a PD meeting a PD meeting? Most of the students had gone home, and only the Belfast people and those committed enough to travel back attended the meeting and took part in the vote. There was also a threat of a

Young Socialist takeover: a section of the Young Socialists didn't want it to be a PD march so that, from then on, they could run the show. But finally the majority decision was, yes, we would march. It was reached in an atmosphere of public hostility—from the press and from other organizations in the civil-rights movement, as well as from the forces of law and order.

On Boxing Day the Minister of Home Affairs—who was now the water-carrying boy scout Captain Long, since the dismissal of Craig earlier in the month—summoned Loudon Seth to see him. Loudon was responsible for coordinating the organization of the march, but as PD was a democratic movement he was not prepared to confront, discuss, or decide as an individual. With only twenty-four hours' notice in the Christmas vacation, it was impossible to call a PD meeting and elect representatives to chat up the Minister. However it was Boxing Night, and I was giving a party at my home in Cookstown for several of the PD faithful. It was decided that those of us present should go with Loudon to Stormont to see Captain Long.

We got the typical Captain Long approach: "Do come in," and apologies for not offering us tea, coffee, and cigarettes, and "How did you enjoy Christmas?" He had a photograph of his son on the desk, and we were entertained to the virtues of Captain Long's son for a while. Then we got down to the discussion. We began by making it clear to Captain Long that we could only state the present position of PD, which was that the march would take place as planned along the route we'd filed for. We could listen to what he had to say, and convey it to the rest of PD, but we could not take any decisions on behalf of PD. Captain Long said he quite understood: it was not his intention to ask us for a decision, but merely to report back on his feelings and those of the police.

He wasn't prepared to make himself unpopular by banning the march, but he did have reservations about it: there were lots of nasty, troublesome people between Belfast and Derry who might not approve of what we were doing, and three or four points were, the police had told him, quite dangerous. We felt that since the police were so well informed ahead of time, they would have plenty of opportunity to cope with the danger. Then a joint press statement was drawn up, by one of us and by a senior civil servant, which gave our agreed account of what had happened at the meeting. Neither Captain Long nor we would make any further public comment, though, as we stressed, we had to report back to our PD mass meeting. Then handshakes all round, and we left Stormont.

I, for one, had been traveling and discussing all day, and most of us had been living since October on cheese sandwiches and a pint of beer at lunchtime and the odd Chinese meal once a week. We decided, on leaving Stormont, that we'd go and have a proper meal. We stopped off at the Globe, a restaurant-cum-bar-cum-pub in Belfast, run by a Roman Catholic Unionist, one Bill O'Hara. And because it was Christmas and we were feeling rich, we decided to end up watching the television news over cups of Gaelic coffee. We were all sitting there peacefully, when Captain Long's photograph flashed on the screen, and the announcer said: "The Minister of Home Affairs today asked the People's Democracy to call off their march in the interests of harmony." The rest of the item suggested that People's Democracy had refused in the interests of peace to do anything

from bad; and we got to Templepatrick and lunchtime in good heart. Then we had a meeting.

The trouble was there were more banners on the march than we'd bargained for. We'd all agreed we'd have a blue civil-rights banner and a black antipoverty banner. Now we discovered we had an anarchist one and a Republican Club one as well. The anarchist banner was hilarious—a great big banner in red and black. But we only had one anarchist. He was big fat John McGuffin, almost as wide as his banner, which he insisted on carrying because, he said, a hundred anarchists were coming from England to march in sympathy with us. So far they hadn't arrived, and while John held up one pole of his banner, the other trailed on the ground. Our detractors said we were a lot of anarchists, but the truth of the matter was not one of us would lift John's other pole. We asked the Republican Club contingent not to carry their banner: for one thing it was larger than the civil-rights banner, and for another it was just not diplomatic to display it. But we said we wouldn't prevent them from carrying it—after all, we believed in freedom. In the end, they compromised: they were prepared to hump their poles and their banner, furled, all the way to Derry on a point of principle.

On we trudged, singing Orange songs, Green songs, red, black, and white songs, and just general pub-crawling and rugby songs, to keep us marching, and the whole tone of the thing at this stage was very good-natured. Already our anarchist, John McGuffin, and doctrinaire Marxist Cyril Toman had fallen out of the march and were riding in the minibus that carried the stores. John was too fat and Cyril had invested in a new pair of mountaineering boots, and the weight and newness of the boots had Cyril's feet destroyed by the time we got to Templepatrick. So the grand theoretician sat in the minibus looking frantically through his Marx to find which part of it dealt with this sort of situation, while the rest of us tittered and laughed and really felt sorry for him.

Occasionally carloads of Paisleyites passed us, shouting, "We'll get you at Knockloughrim!"—a village up the road, which was a well-known citadel of extremism—and this became a joke on the march. When you felt tired, you said, "Keep going—we'll soon be at Knockloughrim." (In fact we never did see Knockloughrim. It was one of the many communities through which the police prevented us from marching.) But in any case we didn't have to travel so far to meet the Paisleyites. They were waiting for us at Antrim, separated from us by a police cordon on Antrim bridge, the first cordon of the march. Beyond the police we could see Major Bunting and his Lambeg drums. The Lambeg drum is a large instrument that beats a dull, thudding, ponderous note, and drumming away there on this mild January afternoon it brought a touch of the jungle to the quiet Ulster countryside.

There was a conference with the police officer in charge, County Inspector Cramsie, whose view, in his strangled Eton-and-Oxford accents, was that our only reasonable course of action was to "go home." Our plan, we told him, was to march through Antrim to a hall on the other side of it where we were to stay the night. No sooner did he know our intentions, than he hopped over the cordon and confided them to Major Bunting. Then back to us to say that, no, we couldn't do what we planned: the Paisleyites weren't in favor. The Paisleyites were illegally blocking the road; there were two policemen for every Paisleyite; Cramsie could easily have dealt with them, but he preferred not to. The chaffering went on, still getting nowhere, and the traffic piled up at both ends of the impasse. We sat down to wait for action. Meanwhile the unceasing pounding of the drums was beginning to get on everyone's nerves, until Wilfie Blackwood, a marcher from Omagh, with a good, loyal Protestant background, broke the tension by jumping up suddenly and shouting, "Hold me back! The drums are getting through!" He made a mad dive at the police cordon, was brought up short, and explained, "It's all right, officer, I'm with the wrong crowd. These civil-rights people had me brainwashed, but the drums are calling me back. I know the color of my skin, I know who are my own people. Let me in to the Major!" On such credentials, the police almost let him through, but he couldn't keep up the comedy, and burst into laughter, so they booted him back among the marchers again.

Then we let Major Bunting come and speak to us. Bunting I have always felt sorry for. He is an ex-soldier who once campaigned for Gerry Fitt. the Republican Labour MP, and he used to be very active against Unionist local councils on behalf of their tenants. Then one day he had a heart attack, and the Reverend Ian Paisley came to him like the ministering angel of God. Bunting saw the light and became a follower of Paisley. He is the military commandant of the movement and, basically because he needs a position of grandeur, he sees himself as a warrior in the cause of justice. Every now and again he breaks down and is ready to give up, but the zeal of the Reverend Paisley keeps him going.

Bunting crossed the cordon and gave us a pretty good civil-rights speech, read a poem, then went back to block the road again, and that was the end of the good community relations bit.

We told the police that we would clear the road to let the traffic through, then march through after it: if they could clear the Paisleyites for the lorries, they could keep them cleared for us. At this the policemen called up reinforcements, and we were forced, quite brutally, into the hedges. I got tramped on a bit, so I called Cramsie over and said, "Do you call yourself an officer, or are you a Paisleyite in disguise?" He told me I was a very impertinent young woman, to which I said, "And you, sir, are a very incompetent old man. If you can't control this force of so-called police, why don't you retire and let somebody who's fit to do the job take over?" Whereupon several policemen dumped me at the edge of the road again with my friends, who produced sedatives, urging, "Bernadette, go on, take half a dozen, but for God's sake, shut up!" "Fair enough," I said, "I'm not saying any more. I'm just going to sit here, and if a policeman comes near me, I'll trip him up as he goes past."

Finally we agreed we'd travel the rest of the way to the hall in police tenders, and moved back down the road to the cheering of the Paisleyites who imagined we were going home. We had planned to eat in Antrim, but with the town closed to us, emergency plans had to be made. By now there were about one hundred and twenty marchers to be fed, and I volunteered to make soup for them with whatever facilities the hall provided. These turned out to be two gas rings, one kettle, and a pan about the size of the average washing machine. Before we left Belfast lots of well-wishers had given us packets of soup, to be made on the "add three quarters of a pint of water" principle, and very few packets were the same sort of soup. Not having much notion of how much soup it takes to feed one hundred and twenty, I filled up the pan with water and, ages later when the water boiled, started emptying in the four-helping packets, counting: "That's four, that's eight, that's twelve . . ." Then it occurred to me that I had no idea how much water the pan held, so there wasn't much point in counting, and finally it got too complicated to try and blend the taste: the chicken went in with the oxtail and the tomato and the vegetable. I just poured them in and kept stirring. That was another difficulty: the only spoon available was a dessertspoon, which kept disappearing into the depths of the pan, and as often as not my whole arm was making the soup. When it was cooked my soup was a thick, dull, stodgy mess, about the consistency of just-made cement. The only thing to do was boil a frantic succession of kettles, serve a dollop of soup-stodge, dilute it, salt and pepper it, and hand it to someone to drink. To complete the catastrophe, our only vessels were plastic coffee beakers which collapsed under the impact of boiling water. "It's worse than the prison ships," people said, but they drank it. Finally the starving masses were rescued by courtesy of the Labour Party who sent fruit and sandwiches.

For the second day of the Long March we were up at six and set off while it was still dark for Randalstown. By this early start we hoped to get through the town before the Paisleyite force, which we had been warned was gathering, reached any strength; but we weren't early enough. Again we were stopped by a police cordon, and again behind the police was a Paisleyite mob. But these were armed—with pickaxes, scythes, saw blades: the most brutal-looking weapons. The general impression was that any marcher who got into Randalstown wouldn't leave it with his head in place.

Fred Taggart and I were sent to ring Harold Wilson. The telephoning of Harold Wilson turned out to be one of the lighter moments in the saga of the march. We knew Harold was no more going to answer the telephone than he was going to appear in person and lead us through Randalstown, but it seemed a gesture anyway, and we planned to ask for the Royal Ulster Constabulary to be replaced by English policemen who would see we got adequate protection on our perfectly legal march to Derry. Fred and I went up to the local curate's house—somewhat warily, for certain of the Catholic clergy had condemned the march. But this curate was all in favor of us, took us in, wouldn't hear of our paying for the call to Downing Street. We got through to some very under-under-undersecretary, and Fred spoke first:

"I want to speak to the Prime Minister."

"You can't speak to the Prime Minister."

"Well, I want the Prime Minister's private secretary."

"Could you tell *me* what the problem is?"

"Yes," said Fred, "I'll tell you what the problem is: here we are marching to Derry, about one hundred and fifty of us, and there are a few policemen blocking the road . . ."

"I'm quite sure, now, the policemen aren't simply obstructing you."

"No, but there's also a mob with scythes and saw blades."

The man at the other end gasped.

"It's quite true," Fred went on, "and people will be killed here, and it will all be Harold Wilson's fault."

"Come, come. You can't blame the Prime Minister for that!"

"I've notified him of it now, and he can't claim he's ignorant of what's going on. If he doesn't do anything about it, by his own inactivity he'll be responsible."

"Well, what do you want done?" asked the man.

"I want an order from the Prime Minister that the road be cleared to let us through."

"I'll put you on to somebody else."

That was the first rung of the ladder cleared. This time I did the talking; then, with the next fellow, Fred; then me. Finally we got up to one of the private secretaries:

"Well, my good man, what's the matter?"

"Don't 'good man' me!" shouts Fred, who had gone through six of them and was sick of telling the story. "Just listen carefully and tell Harold Wilson every word I say. Tell Harold Wilson from me that I will see to it—and all the students here will see to it—that we get to Derry. And if he isn't prepared to do anything, you and I both know there are people not far removed from the spot in Ireland where I'm standing who would be quite willing to clear the way . . ."

"What do you mean?" And Fred just said down the phone, "Have you ever heard of the Irish Republican Army?"

"My good man!" says he, and immediately we got on to someone else who was evidently higher up. Now it was my turn again: "Mr. Taggart here has told you of one sort of assistance we might get, and you all know the Russians are very eager to help people like ourselves in distress . . ."

"Come, now. You're not getting involved with the Russians! It's only a march!" At which Fred grabbed the phone and said, "It might be a bloody only march to you, mate, but there are people here who might be dead by tomorrow, and if one of us is dead, I'm warning you . . ." And he slammed down the phone. So of course we went back. Harold never did anything about it.

Back at the march, everything was as we'd left it, but it had been agreed that the police would lead us by car on a detour round Randalstown. While we waited for the vehicles, we held the trial of County Inspector Cramsie. A judge was elected, and counsel for the prosecution and the defense. Fergus Woods was the only one among us charitable enough to be counsel for the defense, and the plea he made was on the grounds of insanity. His evidence was Cramsie's hat, a sort of Scots piper's forage cap, perched on the side of the head, which, said Fergus, no sane man would wear. Counsel for the prosecution said the hat was, on the contrary, further damning evidence of incompetence, because it was a model for *cadet* county inspectors only. Cramsie was found guilty and sentenced to becoming caretaker of Eton playing fields in perpetuity, and we all enjoyed ourselves watching the policemen in the cordon trying to keep straight faces and Cramsie getting more outraged by the minute, and inviting us to "grow up."

But all the same we were getting restive. The morning was wearing away, and we had got nowhere, and we reckoned that it was deliberate police tactics to stop us and keep us stopped as long as possible, so that we should lose time. Finally the cars arrived, and the police led us off on our detour. But instead of bringing us back to the main road again on the other side of Randalstown, they kept us circling round Northern Ireland for hours. Only when we threatened to stop following them, did they bring us to Toome, the next town on our route. About a mile outside Toome, we assembled, formed up, and marched into the town, the first town of large support. With most of the population marching with us we marched out again—and came up against a police cordon; behind it was the usual gathering of Paisleyites, this time in the company of the brothers Chichester-Clark—Robin, who represents Derry in Westminster, and James Dawson, then Minister of Agriculture, later to become Prime Minister of Northern Ireland. We were still being patient, we were prepared to accept one more reroute from the police. So when they indicated a different road, we took it docilely, and hadn't marched very far up it when we met yet another cordon and yet more Paisleyites. The police, we said, had twenty minutes to clear the Paisleyites: after that we were walking forward. With the town of Toome still in our ranks we outnumbered both police and Paisleyites and for once got our way.

Our program for the rest of the second day was to march through the village of Gulladuff and the town of Maghera to Brackaghreilly, where we were to sleep. It was a long march, we still had twenty miles to do, and, with all the stoppages, we were behind schedule. We walked fast and we ate as we walked, but night was already falling when we reached Gulladuff. The whole village came out to meet us and brought us into the hall where soup and sandwiches in vast quantities had been prepared. They warned us not to go further that evening: the Paisleyites were lying in ambush up the road and it was getting too dark to take them on. By this time there were about six hundred marchers, and the student nucleus was heavily outnumbered by local people who had joined them. Some of the marchers wanted a confrontation with the Paisleyites, and for a moment it looked as if we might not be able to get them to accept our non-violent discipline. But in the end a majority voted to go by car to Brackaghreilly. The villagers of Gulladuff ferried us over in their cars, steering clear of Maghera where the worst concentration of Paisleyites was supposed to be. Later we learned that, foiled of attacking us, they had gone on the rampage in Maghera, sacking, looting, and breaking windows.

We were now some forty miles from Belfast, just over halfway on our journey to Derry. With press, television, and radio reporting on our progress, the march was becoming popular, and in this context there was a real danger that a mob of Paisleyites might attack us while we slept in Brackaghreilly. The police refused us protection, but as it happened we had a much better protective force. When we got to the hall that night, someone said to us, "You make your beds. Bed down for the night. And let none of you walk outside this hall. We will guarantee you perfect safety." To all outward appearances we slept there totally unprotected, but in fact we had shifts of fifty men at a time, armed, guarding the hall. Malachy Carey, one of the marchers, decided that nature was calling and since he couldn't find the bogs, he went out to look for a bush. Just at that point he felt something behind his ear, and a voice said, "Who are you?" "I'm Malachy Carey, one of the marchers," said Malachy, not knowing whether to raise his hands or his trousers. "Oh, that's all right, son," came the voice. "Sorry I disturbed you." That was Brackaghreilly, on Slieve Gallion Mountain, which has always been a Republican stronghold; where the land is bare and poor and the saying is, "You're not a farmer till you've broken Slieve Gallion Mountain": they literally have to break the rock to make any kind of a living.

The third day of the march was to be the longest day, taking in Glenshane Pass, and people were bracing themselves for the extra effort. It turned out to be the best day. Coming up the pass, you can see the mountains and it has the true air of freedom. The way was clear, we were in good territory, and we knew we could march on. Everybody forgot they were tired, forgot Randalstown and Antrim. It was just a fantastic mountain, a fantastic day, great to be free, and we just pounded up the pass. The radio reports on our progress had exclamation marks on them. One hour it was, "The students have reached Glenshane Pass: they should be over it this afternoon." The next bulletin was, "My God, the students have reached the top of the pass! They seem to be running up it! Hardship really makes these young people all the more determined."

At the top of the pass is a pub, called the Ponderosa, a marvelous pub all by itself in the mountains. When we arrived at the Ponderosa it was the only time a democratic decision didn't have to be reached on where we should stop. The march just veered right and descended on the man who owns the pub. He carried half the Ponderosa outside, so that there was room for all of us, everyone had a bottle of something, and we romped on down the pass into the town of Dungiven where we were met by a piper. It was Dungiven's day off. They had been waiting for us to arrive. Women had made sandwiches, local tradesmen had given food, the priest provided cigarettes, the doctor held open surgery for blistered feet, and the municipally owned castle supplied free washing facilities. We paraded the whole town —as if we hadn't far enough to walk—and the people lined the streets and cheered. There was only one sad note: the two schools, Catholic and Protestant, are quite close together. As we passed the Catholic school, shouting "Free day for the schools!" the children all came tumbling out, scrambling over the school gate to join us, and teachers were running around with canes, going thump! thump! getting them all back into classrooms. Finally there was a cordon of teachers at the gate, roaring at the children, telling them that they could stand and watch, but must go back to their lessons when the march had passed. At the Protestant school there were a few wistful faces at the windows and the stern face of a teacher pushing the children back in. And sheer silence.

Outside Dungiven there's a fork: both roads lead to Derry. Our route was planned for the left fork, through the towns of Feeny and Claudy, but the police wanted us to take the other one, the more direct road, missing out Feeny, which, they said, was hostile territory. Now we had got pretty tired of the police telling us of the mobs of Paisleyites up the road, and we'd decided that they were being a bit too successful in keeping us out of the towns along our route. So while the rest of us started marching, Nuala Stewart and Malachy Carey went up the Feeny-Claudy road by car hunting for Paisleyites; and found none. They got back to find the march, now a thousand strong, yet once more brought to a halt by a police cordon. They left the car on the other side of the cordon, walked through to rejoin us, and reported that the only people they had met on the road were three children coming home from school. We had a meeting: were we going to accept another reroute? Our pacifists said, "Let us sit in the road till the cordon goes away." Our militants said, "The great appear great because we are on our knees: let us arise." And most of us said, "Let us walk through the cordon."

We agreed on procedure: arms linked, heads down, keep a steady pace, one-two, one-two; no matter what happened you were to keep walking. If the person beside you fell, you were to hang on to him and trail him along till he could regain his balance. If a person was knocked unconscious, you were not to let go but use him simply as body weight. So we started off, arms linked, heads down, one-two, one-two, and we were up to the cordon. The police had also linked arms, and they started pushing. One of the radio channels had a reporter there: "And the marchers are now approaching the police cordon. The police have forced them back. No! The marchers are forcing themselves forward! Yes, yes! The police are moving back! No, the cordon is holding tight! Yes! The marchers are back! Forward! Back! Forward! Back! My God! The marchers are through! They're *all* through! There are policemen in the ditch! The marchers are pouring through, they're just running up the road. They've gone through!" It was like a rugby match.

In fact there weren't many policemen there, about one hundred and fifty or so, and the whole thing was rather half-hearted. I was one of three girls in the front line, and we came up against three big burly policemen, one of whom said, "Ah now, girls, this is no place for you. Move you into the back line for we don't want to fight girls."

"Well, we're not going to fight at all," I said, "but I'll tell you what to do. The way you play this game is—you push and we push, and whoever pushes the hardest is the winner."

"I'm not fighting women," he said, and broke the cordon. Perhaps he thought we would feel belittled and break our line too, but we just trampled over him to the next row of police, and pushed them all into the ditch. I pulled a muscle in my leg holding a policeman's weight on my arm while the other marchers got through. Our line had pushed them into the ditch, and this particular man was sitting rather ridiculously on top of some other policemen, and he kept lunging to get up. To keep him sitting down and helpless

I had to brace myself against the ditch and press my head against my arm on his waist. But nobody was hurt.

Once through the cordon we went up the Feeny road at a tremendous lick, fearing that the police might come after us, or that a new cordon might form up ahead, trapping us between two forces. They did in the end appear, but only to escort us. They lined the sides of the march and brought up the rear in tenders. We were, at least, being taken seriously. Through Feeny, into Claudy, where people arrived feeling exhausted but modestly triumphant, for we were almost home, Derry was only ten miles away. For many of us, the first drink of the march, apart from our visit to the Ponderosa, was bought in Claudy. After that there was a long and hectic meeting, but I knew nothing about it: I got back to the hall we were to stay in, found my two blankets, rolled up in them where I found them near the door, and just lay there being walked over by people all night.

There was trouble in Derry that night. The Paisleyites held a meeting in the Guildhall there, and the people of Derry assembled outside it and could only be cleared by baton charges by the police. Major Bunting's car was overturned and set alight. Next morning, for the last lap of the Long March, we had a late start. The events in Derry the night before had shown how near the surface violence was, and we feared we might not be able to control the feelings of the nonstudent majority of the marchers. A meeting was called and Michael Farrell addressed it. We had shown we could make our point by nonviolent demonstration, he said, and he begged anybody who felt, justifiably or not, that he couldn't follow the nonviolent principle, not to march with us. The expression Farrell used was "no retaliation should be offered except where danger to life or limb is likely to be occasioned in the immediate instance." It all sounded great, and everybody agreed that only if their heads were actually coming off would they retaliate. We set off at a kind of weary, healthy trudge—pleased to be arriving, but feeling that it was a bit of an anticlimax nonetheless. At the road junction at Cumber, there were the police.

As usual, there were Paisleyites up ahead, but under the new conditions of escorting the march, the police would take us through. They expected stones to be thrown three hundred yards up the road; they couldn't guarantee our safety; but if we insisted on going, they would do their best. We were held up, while the police went up to reconnoiter the area. Off they went on their reconnoiter, and they reconnoitered back with no more information than before they started. Probably they were going up there to tell the Paisleyites how many of us there were, and what we planned to do. Then the police donned helmets and riot shields, turned up their collars and got out their batons. Most of them rode in the tenders. The others walked beside the march. We covered our heads with anything we had, turned up our collars, linked arms—again to carry along anybody who got clonked on the head—and kept in to the right side of the road, with our heads down, keeping a steady pace and waiting for the first stone to fall. I was walking between Gerry Lawless and a self-confessed coward, Eddie Toman. Eddie was saying that if stones did come, he was going to throw himself under me and he hoped I didn't expect any protection on the grounds that I was a female. Lawless's view was that men and women are equal: you look after yourself, Devlin, if anything happens, because I'm scarpering. So there I was, flanked by two excellently chivalrous gentlemen, with the prospect of protecting both of them if anything happened. Another girl was in my line. For a while she braved it: no Paisleyite was going to make her walk with her head down. But we urged, "Look, it's not a matter of pride, it's a matter of efficiency. If you walk with your head down, you'll walk further. Walk with your head up and you mightn't have an eye when the stone lands." In this kind of tense, yet farcical, atmosphere we trudged up the road, waiting for the stones to come pouncing over.

Three hundred yards. Not a thing happened. Four hundred, five hundred, six hundred yards—and not a solitary stone. We were walking in beside the hedge, beyond which the ground rose steeply above us. Through the spaces in the hedge root could be seen at regular intervals neatly organized piles of stones and neatly arranged rows of bottles, alternating with each other. And we could see policemen and Paisleyites. The policemen marching with us were equipped for battle, but the policemen on the other side of the hedge were dressed for traffic duty, and they were chatting amiably to the men they were moving back. We went on walking: half a mile, three quarters of a mile; the odd stone came flying over.

And then we came to Burntollet Bridge, and from lanes at each side of the road a curtain of bricks and boulders and bottles brought the march to a halt. From the lanes burst hordes of screaming people wielding planks of wood, bottles, laths, iron bars, crowbars, cudgels studded with nails, and they waded into the march beating the hell out of everybody.

I was a very clever girl: cowardice makes you clever. Before this onslaught, our heads-down, arms-linked tactics were no use whatever, and people began to panic and run. Immediately my mind went back to Derry on October 5 and I remembered the uselessness of running. As I stood there I could see a great big lump of flatwood, like a plank out of an orange-box, getting nearer and nearer my face, and there were two great nails sticking out of it. By a quick reflex action, my hand reached my face before the wood did, and immediately two nails went into the back of my hand. Just after that I was struck on the back of the knees with this bit of wood which had failed to get me in the face, and fell to the ground. And then my brain began to tick. "Now, Bernadette," I said, "what is the best thing to do? If you leave your arms and legs out, they'll be broken. You can have your skull cracked, or your face destroyed." So I rolled up in a ball on the road, tucked my knees in, tucked my elbows in, and covered my face with one hand and the crown of my head with the other. Through my fingers, I could see legs standing round me: about six people were busily involved in trying to beat me into the ground, and I could feel dull thuds landing on my back and head. Finally these men muttered something incoherent about leaving that one, and tore off across the fields after somebody else.

When everything was quiet, and five seconds had gone by without my feeling anything, I decided it was time to take my head up. I had a wee peer round, ducked again as a passing Paisleyite threw a swipe at me, and then got up. What had been a march was a shambles. The first few rows had managed to put a spurt on when the attack came, had got through the ambush and were safely up the road. The rest of us were all over the place. The attackers were beating marchers into the ditches, and across the ditches into the river. People were being dragged half-conscious out of the river. Others were being pursued across the fields into the woods. Others had been trapped on the road and were being given a good hiding where they stood. As I got shakily to my feet and looked round, I saw a young fellow getting a thrashing from four or five Paisleyites, with a policeman looking on: the policeman was pushing the walking-wounded marchers up the road to join the front rows and doing nothing to prevent the attack. "What the bloody hell d'you think you're doing?" I shouted at him, whereupon he gave me a vigorous shove and said, "Get up the road to the rest of your mates, you stupid bitch." (Policemen always call me a stupid bitch, and I deny that I'm stupid.) Well, that push was enough for me, unsteady as I was: I just went sprawling right into Maurice Keenan, one of the marchers, and another policeman; and Bernadette's passive mood changed to anger. Maurice got me back on my feet again, saying, "Now take it easy," and even the other policeman protested to the fellow who had pushed me, "Mind the way you throw those kids about; they're getting enough." He was quite reasonable: "Go you right up and stay with the march," he said to me, "and we'll get the rest of your friends."

As I turned to walk away, an unconscious girl who was bleeding about the head somewhere was carried by two of the marchers to a police truck, and the constable in the truck pushed her away with his foot. "She must get to the hospital," said the marchers, pushing her in. "Take her to the hospital yourself," said the constable, pushing her out. At that, two other officers came over and threw *him* out of the truck. "For Christ's sake, let the child in," they said. A few policemen were at least trying to stop us from being killed, but the others were quite delighted that we were getting what, in their terms, we deserved.

I went rampaging up the road saying that if I had my way, not one solitary policeman who was at Burntollet would live to be sorry for what he had done; that there was only one way of dealing with the police force—give them three weeks for every honest man to get out of it, then systematically shoot the rest. The policeman who had shoved me kept pace: "You say that again and you're for it! Say stuff like that again you'll find yourself in the tender!" And I kept on saying it, and so we kept up this barrage all the way up the road.

Back with what was left of the march, I found that Tom McGurk, well-known moderate of the PD, was arguing for the march to be stopped, and everyone else was quite willing to make a sacrifice of him to the Paisleyites; for how do you stop anything in the middle of a riot? I was frantically looking round for people I couldn't see. The last time I'd seen Gerry Lawless, he'd been scrambling over a ditch having the head thumped off him by four Paisleyites, and I thought he had probably been killed. And I couldn't find Eddie Toman: these were my two "cowards," and they were both missing. I found Eamonn McCann: "Look, Eamonn, I'll have to go back to look for people." Eamonn said, "If we get out of this without having at least three people dead, we shall thank God, if he exists, for miracles; but if you go down there, there'll be four people dead; and when you don't come back, *I'll* go down there and I'll be dead; and it will all be lovely. All we can do is march on and hope we don't find a corpse when we get to Derry." And that was the first thing that really brought me to my senses. There were, as it happened, no deaths, but eighty-seven people were taken to hospital from Burntollet, and many more were less seriously injured. No one was brought to justice for it, nor ever will be. Evidence was collected—by civilians, not by the police who didn't see the necessity for doing so; individuals were named;

but Major Chichester-Clark, when he became Prime Minister, declared an amnesty, and our attackers need never worry about the damage they did us at Burntollet Bridge.

So we marched on. That was a very moving point of the march: there were cows in the fields, munching away totally undisturbed; the whole countryside was peaceful, still, quiet; and there we were trudging up the road, battered and bruised, singing "We shall overcome—some day." But that song was too resigned, so we resorted to the "Internationale," and it was never sung with more fervor than coming away from Burntollet Bridge. That was our strong point: we had faced the attack without fighting back, and we had come out of it singing.

As we approached Derry, we were met by the Radical Students' Alliance who had come out to meet us. They stood to attention, singing the "Internationale" with us, as we went past, then fell in to form the end of the march. They were the only people who did this: other supporters joining us forced their way into our ranks, but the Radical Students paid this homage to those of us who had come all the way from Belfast. The police had promised us more trouble before we reached the city center, and as we drew level with the first houses, Eamonn McCann got up on a chair to call through a megaphone: "Remember we have marched seventy-three miles. Please don't let violence mar the end of the march. If you're attacked, just keep marching." The march went by, Eamonn was left there all on his own, and a wee Paisleyite ran out and thumped him; so Eamonn, of course, took to his heels and ran and found the rest of the march again. We came abreast of Altnagelvin Hospital, and all our people who could hobble out, hobbled into the front rows with their bandages, and so, two thousand strong, we rounded the corner and came down the hill to the walled city of Derry.

A bonfire was waiting for us in Irish Street, to burn such of our banners as had survived Burntollet Bridge. Again the march was met by a rain of stones, bricks, bottles, burning sticks from the bonfire, and petrol bombs. Fortunately the Paisleyites were very bad at making petrol bombs—most of the ones they threw simply didn't materialize. I could feel stones bouncing off my head, leaving me apparently undamaged, and I saw four hit Michael Farrell before he fell: he carries his blood-stained coat around with him to this day for the prestige of it. Farther down the road a squad of Paisleyites had got into a quarry behind the houses and were lobbing stones over the roofs. The police advised us to wait until the enemy ran out of ammunition, and this looked like being a long wait, for they had ammunition there for the next ten years. The marchers stood in against the houses to avoid the stones, which were coming flying over into the middle of the street, and overshooting to break windows in the houses opposite. Every time there was a lull, a few more marchers sprinted to safety, and bit by bit we all got past.

That was the last danger: now we were in Derry, and the people lined the streets and cheered. They'd put up a platform in Guildhall Square, and they wanted all of us on it at once: every time a few more were dragged up one side, several fell off at the other side. But the people wanted to hear something from all of us. That was when I called Derry "the capital city of injustice"—grand phrase: it flashed all over Ireland. It was impossible to describe the atmosphere, but it must have been like that on V-Day: the war was over and we had won; we hadn't lifted a finger, but we'd won.

Chapter 10

Basically, I think, lots of us just wanted to sit down and cry with relief. After I'd made my little speech on the platform, I went into the City Hotel with Eamonn McCann, and we were sitting there, quietly drinking whiskey, when a friend came in: "Bernadette, I must see you; come upstairs." I was too tired to argue, so I trotted after him. There was a doctor upstairs who took my pulse.

"Yes, you need a rest."

"She needs sedatives," said my escort. Two tablets were issued to me and a glass of water, and I was shut into one of the hotel bedrooms for an hour's rest. I lay down on the bed, but the mixture of whiskey and sedative, instead of relaxing me, began making the room go round. The clock in Guildhall Square started to chime, the booming pounded against my head, and everything that had happened on the march was going through my brain. I kept wondering if people were lying dead at Burntollet Bridge, and I became convinced I'd been locked in by someone who didn't want me to go back to Burntollet and discover the truth. After trying the door, I sat down on the bed and started to cry.

While I was still sobbing someone unlocked the door and half-seeing, half-drunk, and half-drugged, I went tottering down the corridor in my bare feet. Then I heard someone else weeping: I opened the door, went in and found another girl who had been given sedatives and reduced to a state of hysterics. She didn't know where she was, she'd missed a lift back to Dublin, and she was in total disarray. This sobered me up. I found the people who were meant to be taking her to Dublin and sorted her out. Then I told the sedative-prescribers what I thought of them: this sort of chat suggested I was my old self again, and I was given leave to wander about as I pleased.

That evening I was due in Dublin myself to do a program on Radio Telefis Eireann with Tom McGurk and John McGuffin. The taxi man was terrified of taking us: there were rumors that the Paisleyites were felling trees and blocking roads to keep us all bottled up in Derry. But finally he took his courage in his hands and we traveled to Dublin quite peacefully, except that the little man on the border recognized us: "Were you the young girl making the speeches in Derry?" he asked. I said I was. "Well," he said, "it's just as well you're heading home."

We got back to Queen's midway through January 1969, and the hundred or so of us who had completed the whole march were, by reason of our experiences between Belfast and Derry, a lot more politically aware than we had been when we started out. We had moved from vague socialism to committed socialism. It may sound strange that simply marching and getting thumped on the head and being fed by people do this kind of thing to you, but it is true that our experiences on the Long March gave the once nonideological PD a strongly left-wing hard core of people who stuck together.

Beyond the hard core there was a large number of socialist-orientated people, who usually turned up to meetings, as well as one or two unpolitical, well-meaning individuals who were still frightened of socialism. Because of the mass-democracy structure of PD—because there was no formal membership, no political line that everybody had to toe—it was theoretically possible for antisocialists to pack a meeting and swing a policy vote their way. But the general drift was decidedly to the left.

We then agreed that there was no point in our working on parallel lines with the Civil Rights Association, and large numbers of us joined it—not as the PD, but as individuals. On our side it was a genuine attempt to forge a unity between the two different bodies and put our weight as effectively as possible behind the civil-rights cause. We weren't interested in PD power, and we accepted that in the CRA we wouldn't have the open-speaking rights that we had in our own organization, but we also realized that the PD structure wouldn't work outside student society: at town level, you couldn't hold mass meetings every night, you needed a secretary and a treasurer and a committee to prepare policy. However the PD influx into the CRA was seen by existing members as a sinister takeover plot, and hostility came to a head at the CRA's annual general meeting early in the year.

When the Civil Rights Association was founded in 1966, it consisted of not just random people, but of representatives of every political party in Northern Ireland, including the Unionists (who subsequently resigned from it). Its executive have always been respectable, middle-class people, who probably started out from the feeling that something was wrong in society and should be put right, but whose demands have since hardened into a campaign for Catholic equality. Until the 1969 annual general meeting, the chairman of the association was Betty Sinclair, one of Northern Ireland's handful of Communist Party members and a true old-guard reactionary. In her time Betty had done good work for the trade unions in Northern Ireland, but her main activity as chairman of the CRA seemed to be sending telegrams to Harold Wilson. The time was never right for action. Whatever was proposed, and however the proposal was received by the rest of the executive, for Betty it was always, "The time is not right for action."

Betty was ousted at the annual general meeting, and was very hurt, for you don't oust your masters every day of the week. Immediately she launched an attack on the PD, specifically on Michael Farrell and myself. This didn't work, but merely alienated Betty, and we were delighted: by alienating herself, she gave us an opportunity to push the Communists out of the civil-rights movement, which we felt was important because the Communists, particularly in Northern Ireland, are as reactionary as the Unionists. The new chairman was Frank Gogarty, and he was joined on the executive by two PD members, Michael Farrell and Kevin Boyle. Thereafter things became generally more liberal within the CRA. In the past the CRA had no active function, apart from issuing statements and providing speakers and generally pulling the various parts of the civil-rights movement together. Although it had largely got the credit for all the demonstrations that happened in Northern Ireland, it had in fact organized very few of them. But now it began working on PD-type activities.

And here the PD made a major mistake. Though we were having an effect on the Civil Rights Association, the CRA was also having an effect on us. To preserve the unity with the CRA, we arrested the socialist development of People's Democracy. We became satisfied with pushing our views through the CRA. We didn't call attention to the glaring discrepancy between the CRA's demand of a fair allocation (on religious lines) of jobs and houses, and our demand of jobs and houses for everyone. We should have made our policies felt much more strongly. We should have produced a newspaper for education purposes. We should have started campaigns on the specific issues of low wages and unemployment, and gone in for mass squatting of the homeless in empty property. We didn't have a retreat from militancy, but in the interests of unity, we didn't step our militancy up. While all these things were failing to happen, the Prime Minister of Northern Ireland, Captain Terence O'Neill, announced we were to have a general election.

Our long march to Derry had been followed by a month of demonstrations, counterdemonstrations, violence, tough government measures—and a crisis in the Unionist Party. Three members of the government resigned in the last week of January and a section of the Unionist MP's signed a statement demanding a change of leadership. On February 2, the Reverend Ian Paisley led six thousand supporters through Belfast, calling for O'Neill's head, and Captain Terence decided there was nothing for it but to go to the country. There would be a general election on February 24—not to decide on policies, but to settle the squabbles in the Unionist Party: it was a clear demonstration that Captain O'Neill and all the other members of the government thought that the good of the party and the good of the country were one and the same thing.

We in the PD decided that the whole election was a farce: in the middle of the civil-rights movement, we were being treated to the old, flag-waving traditions of "Up the border!" and "Down the border!" Such was the depth of political thought put into the election by the politicians. In any case, we felt, the Unionist Party's squabbles were no concern of the people as a whole.

In Northern Ireland, there used to be only two main parties, Unionists and Nationalists, and if there was a sufficient majority of either Protestants or Catholics in a constituency, the seat was never contested. We picked eight such constituencies and took on both parties on a nonsectarian platform of radical policies. It was our golden opportunity. We didn't want to get into Parliament, but here was the chance we'd been waiting for to explain our policies to the people. The police were bound by law to protect a parliamentary candidate; we could send an election manifesto into every home in eight constituencies, with the Post Office paying for our propaganda; and as candidates, we could attack the political parties at meetings to which electors came. People laughed at us: "Whoever heard of students going to the country?" That didn't work: we were quite unmoved. Then they accused us of trying to jump on the political bandwagon and of being power and glory hunters. But they couldn't make the accusation convincing, for we were fighting seats that nobody had contested for forty years, seats we had no chance of winning.

In this election there was in most constituencies a three-cornered fight, and after years of voting along unalterable religious lines, the electorate was delighted. You had not only someone to fight the Unionists, but you had Official Unionists, Unofficial Unionists, Official Unofficial Unionists, with Protestant Unionists thrown in for good measure. The whole Unionist population could toss two pennies and work out by permutation whom it was voting for. And on the Opposition side, you could vote Nationalist, Northern Ireland Labour, Republican Labour, National Democrat, Liberal, People's Progressive Party, People's Democracy. It was a whole political confusion in response to the election.

We were the only people who had a policy, and though we were contemptuous of the election, we played it according to the rules better than anybody else. We canvassed at doors, explained our beliefs, and asked people to give us their votes. Nobody else bothered: they just stuck to their slogans. "The civil-rights movement will destroy the border—vote Unionist"; or "Captain O'Neill is selling us down the river— vote Protestant Unionist"; or "The Unionist Party is falling apart at the seams—vote Official Unionist"; or "Faith of our fathers—vote Nationalist."

I contested South Derry against Major James Dawson Chichester-Clark, then Minister of Agriculture but shortly to be Prime Minister of Northern Ireland. The Major, in my opinion, has always been the nigger in the Unionist woodpile. His constituency, South Derry, consists of such places as the 100 per cent Protestant town of Tobermore; as the village of Knockloughrim, where we were threatened with destruction; as the village of Upperlands through which no Fenian passes; as the districts of Bovagh and Bovedy, where you wear your orange lily on your sleeve if you want to get through alive: real, primitive Paisleyite country, and their representative in Parliament is Major Chichester-Clark. During the election campaign, every Unionist candidate was crossexamined by his constituents as to where he stood on O'Neill and Paisley; and if he was pro-O'Neill, a Protestant Unionist or an anti-O'Neill Unionist opposed him. The Major never said where he stood; but the Major was not, in fact, opposed. For a moment it looked as if he might be: at five minutes to the deadline on nomination day, a wee man strolled in with his nomination papers and was told they needed adjustment. The adjustment would have taken him three minutes to make. But at five minutes past the deadline, he was still struggling with them. I heaved a sigh of relief—if he'd got his papers in, in time, it was quite feasible that the Unionist vote would have been split, and I would have found myself in Stormont. Major Chichester-Clark heaved a rather dubious sigh of relief, as if to say, "I thought for one moment he was going to double-cross me and actually put those papers in." And that gave a touch of reality to the whole situation. Through all the trouble and recriminations in the Unionist Party, he was on good terms with the Paisleyites, and when he became Prime Minister, the Reverend Ian Paisley said, "All is well."

In the course of his campaign, the Major made not one election speech. He went off quietly at one stage to London, and we commented, "He's the next prime minister. He's testing his ground, sitting on the fence so that he doesn't offend anybody." Nobody knew whether he was for O'Neill or against him, for reform or against it. Full-page advertisements appeared in all the newspapers: the only one Chichester-Clark was in was the list of official Unionist candidates. He wasn't in the list supporting O'Neill; he wasn't in the list opposing O'Neill. He was in nothing. Just the quiet nonexistent candidate who won the election and the leadership.

On election night, I met the Major at the count in Coleraine. There was an electorate of some eighteen thousand in South Derry, of whom fifteen thousand voted. Just over nine thousand voted for him, and just under six thousand voted for me; and the good Major got greener with every hundred votes that came up. Early in the day I said to him,

"May the best woman win!" but the remark was too subtle for the gentleman, it went right over his head; and he still didn't seem to get it when I shook hands with him that night and said, "Well, the best woman won."

That was one of our best results. Our great victory was in South Down, a previously uncontested Nationalist seat. The Nationalist who had held the seat for years got back into Parliament against an unemployed graduate, Fergie Woods, but Fergie lost by fewer than 250 votes, and the country was in an uproar. The parties went wild: "If the students get away with this . . ." We had fought on the policies of the civil-rights movement and clear-cut socialism, and the people came out in Northern Ireland and voted for them.

Not everyone in PD was in favor of our fighting the election. Since January, the general move to the left had been paralleled by the emergence of other ideological trends in the bosom of PD. Whereas once it had been hard to tell one unpolitical student from another, now people could get up at meetings to offer solutions, saying, "I'm a Liberal and I believe . . ." or "I'm a Unionist and I believe . . ." or more likely, "I'm a socialist and I believe . . ." But the more socialist and the more determined PD grew, the fewer its numbers became, and though we still had massive support in February, the decision to fight the election began the decline in numbers. Opposition came on two fronts: from the doctrinaire anarchist and ultrasocialist people, who said elections were bourgeois and shouldn't be touched; and from a sectarian element who were quite happy that PD should stand against the Unionists but kicked up hell about PD standing against the Nationalists, thus splitting the Opposition vote. (And we did do this: mainly thanks to us, the Nationalists lost three of the nine seats they held in Stormont.)

One of our aims when we sent our teams into the eight constituencies was to set up local PD-type bodies in them, so spreading our beliefs through the country. The most successful of these ventures was created by Cyril Toman in Armagh, where attacks against the local authority were so hard-hitting that the council began holding its meetings behind locked doors with the police on guard to keep the PD away. Another lively body started working in Fermanagh and there were others in Bannside (where Michael Farrell had contested the seat against O'Neill and Paisley), and South Derry. This decentralization worked—but it worked to the disadvantage of the original PD in Belfast, which now found itself a shrinking part of a larger movement. Not only were the activists and the thinkers traveling down to the provincial PD's to nurse them into strength, so losing touch with events in Belfast; but for the mainly student members of the Belfast PD, final examinations were beginning to loom above the horizon and they were turning from politics to studying. The PD lost what it had once had—a solid movement of people who took action and a well-attended discussion forum for the development of ideas. The PD still met, it still talked, but such action as was taken at this time was initiated by the local branches, and, within the Civil Rights Association, the PD began to lose its identity.

A march was planned for Easter. Originally it was to have been a Belfast-London march, but that idea was scrubbed in favor of a march to Dublin. In principle this was a good idea, because it would show that the system PD was complaining about existed in the South of Ireland as well as in the North. But the timing was wrong: the march, starting from Belfast on Holy Thursday, was due to reach Dublin at Easter and would inevitably get all mixed up with the people celebrating the Easter Rising and claiming credit for setting up the Republic. By this time I had got involved in the Mid-Ulster by-election campaign and wasn't attending PD meetings in Belfast, but I went with Loudon Seth and Eamonn McCann to Galway, in the Republic of Ireland, and got the students there to march to Dublin to meet the PD. The march was held, it ran into trouble from the police at Lurgan, but the protest misfired and our issues became utterly confused with the censorship and contraceptive controversies in the South.

By the beginning of the summer term, only the really committed people still attended meetings regularly and worked for PD. The time for marching was over and there just weren't enough people to carry out all the kinds of meaningful action properly. Then the PD produced its newspaper. This was an idea we'd had months earlier but had never put into effect. At the general election we brought out a "Why PD?" newssheet, explained the existence, aims, and policies of the movement. It was hoped this would be followed by a regular newssheet at fortnightly intervals, but nothing appeared until June when people felt that it was four months too late: it would have been more useful when PD was a larger movement, centered on Belfast.

But the big weakness of the PD—as of other student organizations—is that generations are short, people go away in vacations to work in London or somewhere, and the few who remain behind develop politically beyond all the rest. When student enthusiasm was at its height, we should have put a structure on the organization so that when one lot of students moved out, the structure would have remained for another lot to move into. However, efficiency doesn't only depend on numbers and the PD nucleus has continued—and perhaps can continue—to work in the context of the Civil Rights Association.

Over the months, the CRA has moved in a natural progression from demanding something for the minority (that is, the Catholics); to demanding Catholic equality; to demanding Catholic power. This has been better appreciated by the Paisleyites, who are in no doubt that it is a Catholic movement, than by the civil-rights supporters. Because events happened so quickly at the end of 1968 and the beginning of 1969, and because of the repressive reaction of the government and police, the CRA, which had been a not very effective pressure group, suddenly found itself a sort of spokesman for a popular movement consisting of very disparate elements indeed. Most people only knew that something was wrong, and hoped that if they marched enough and protested enough, the press or television reporters or public opinion generally would take note and somehow put the wrong thing right; but they had no clear idea of how this was to be done, and they weren't politically educated enough to appreciate the gaping abyss between the Catholic-rights line of the CRA and the rights-of-the-underprivileged-in-general line of more militant parts of the movement, such as PD. If this *had* been appreciated, the splits which began to appear in the movement in the summer of 1969 would have shown themselves very much earlier on. However, there was never anything blatantly sectarian in the movement. The slogan was "We are nonpolitical, nonsectarian," and if you prefaced your remarks with that, you could get away with pretty well anything.

The danger was that as the Catholic-rights line developed, what had started out as a generous (though vague) protest on behalf of the oppressed began turning into an all-class alliance of Catholics, happy if it achieved no more than

Catholic control of predominantly Catholic areas. In this sort of situation, you had Catholic slum landlords marching virtuously beside the tenants they exploited, Catholic employers marching in protest against the Protestants they excluded from their factories. The main reason why this happened was that elements in the leadership had their own interests at heart. These leaders had no intention of pushing the civil-rights demand to its logical conclusion of bringing down an unjust government: what they wanted was majority rule in Catholic areas—where they would be the rulers. This achieved, the system could remain precisely what it was and the civil-rights movement disband: for the grievance of the middle-class Catholic in Ulster is that he's not a first-class citizen. His demand, the Unionist government can satisfy without much inconvenience, but the demand of the working-class Catholic—that, irrespective of religion, fathers and husbands should be able to live and work in Ireland with decent wages and something like human dignity— would, if it were granted, break the Unionist government's back.

Where the PD made its mistake was in not seeing soon enough that identification with such policies was too high a price to pay for the unity of the civil-rights movement. Just at the point where we were breaking through as a socialist force, we back-pedaled on socialism to keep the movement together, and by losing our identity within what was regarded as a Catholic movement, we only made more difficult for ourselves the almost insuperable problem of enlisting the support of the Protestant working class. If we get the Protestant working class on our side, the fun will really start. In the past, the difficulty of getting Protestant support has always been the drawback of Irish movements, but when the difficulty has been overcome, the Protestant working class has proved more militant, more radical, more determined; and it has in the end been the Catholics who gave in to the Church's pressures in favor of the status quo.

But how to get through to the Protestants? If Paisley had never existed, it would have been much easier, for he has played on their fear that their heritage is threatened—and for this the Unionists tolerate Paisley: he serves the purpose of keeping their boys in line. The Protestant working man doesn't support the Unionist government as such—he supports it because he sees it as the Protestant parliament. He isn't really interested in being British. The average Irish Catholic will claim his nationality is Irish and be done with it; the average Protestant will claim he's British, but all the same, his hatred for the Englishman is almost greater than the Catholic's. For the Ulster Protestant feels he is an inferior English citizen. We don't feel that—we don't want to be English citizens of any variety. But he feels he must continually prove he's British. He must flaunt his Union Jack, he must have his picture of the Queen. It's as though he were saying, "We *are* British . . . aren't we?" But if it came to a conflict between being British and being an Ulster Protestant, every last one of them would forsake their British heritage. They would miss the Queen, but there is nothing else they would miss.

But the Protestant workingman has a different, and more sinister, possibility ahead of him. Even the Unionist Party is getting tired of being led by the landed gentry, and the coming batch of leaders—men like William Craig, Brian Faulkner, Paul Taylor—have much stronger roots in the working class. They see themselves as the saviors of Ulster Protestantism. If they get their way, Northern Ireland, with a much more working-class parliament, may find itself drifting toward a sort of national socialism. There would be state-owned factories, but no "disloyal elements" would be employed in them, and you might quite easily see a mass movement of Catholics out of the country: it could be something akin to Hitler and the Jews.

If this doesn't happen and we can remove the fear that we are trying to destroy Ulster Protestantism, our worst problem will be solved. This has already been done in a small way and at a local level by concentrating on specific issues and demonstrating that our action does not harm, but benefits, the working class. In Armagh, and particularly in Derry, where civil-rights groups squatted homeless people in empty houses, you find Protestant families who say, "Well, I still don't agree with those civil rights, but what you're doing now is good." Once get through to them like that, and they would be the first to haul down the Union Jack and up with the Starry Plough; and the good Ulster Catholics will have a job keeping up with them, for Mother Church will then be on all our heels screaming about the Red Flag.

The first warnings from the Church were, in fact, sounded as far back as January 1969, when the Long March was in progress. In spite of the opposition we were facing, the parish priest of Antrim got up in the pulpit one good Christian Sunday and said no sensible Catholic should give us help. Later Cardinal Conway, who is Bishop of Armagh, Primate of All Ireland, and a liberal fellow in private, painted a dishonest picture of our movement to scare the pants off any

Catholic followers we might have. Marxists, he said, tell you of the free and equal man in the socialist state, but look around at your actual socialist states, and you find man in a greater state of slavery, having lost more of his personality, under greater penalties, than anywhere else. The Cardinal knew perfectly well the difference between Communists and socialists, and that the Marxist theory propagated in Northern Ireland had been strongly anti-Communist. But the Church in Ireland is so conservative that it still believes there's no room for religion in a socialist country. In a socialist Ireland there would be room for the Church—unless the Church dug its heels in, as in the past, and pitted its influence against the march of events.

What at this stage we need is an organization—a clearly socialist organization with defined aims and policies—which would spread and develop specific local action. By our insistence that we weren't party-political, we've built up a resistance among our followers to an orthodox political party, trying to get representation in Parliament and so forth, but within the mass civil-rights movement there is an opportunity to develop an organization to campaign on specific problems like low wages and unemployment.

What we must at all times make clear is that we are fighting for the economic rights of an underprivileged people, not to win back the Six Counties for Ireland. Economically, I believe, the South of Ireland is worse off than we are, and I would hope that as we step up the struggle in Ulster, there will be those in the South who would step up the struggle there. This is maybe just ideological talk. It will take a long time to achieve anything. And in the end, I believe, it will come to a clash—for at no time have those in authority relinquished their position without a struggle. But when it comes to that, it must be fought not in the Six Counties by Catholics, but in Ireland as a whole by the working class. Only if it's an all-Ireland working-class revolution, are there enough of us to overthrow the powers that be.

Chapter 11

I didn't want to stand for election to Westminster. I didn't
know anything about Parliament, I'd never been inside the
House of Commons, and I found Stormont a total farce. Of
formal politics, I was—and am—totally ignorant. It is nothing
to my academic credit that when people start sorting out the
Bolsheviks from the Mensheviks, I can't follow the arguments. I know they fought in the Russian Revolution, but
God alone knows what they did there. And as for parliamentary politics in the West, I didn't respect the system and,
even if I had, that wasn't the sort of politician I wanted to be.
My whole experience of "tuppence-ha'penny politicians in
the tuppence-ha'penny state" of Northern Ireland suggested
that getting into Parliament meant the loss of honesty and
integrity. And moral considerations apart, I just didn't have
the shrewdness that plays off one politician against another,
supporting a colleague in something you only half believe in
to commit him to supporting you next time around. This is
how Parliament really works: you sign my bit of paper for
this motion, and I'll sign yours for the next, and we'll agree
to differ on the one following. But I can't do this kind of

thing—I just open my mouth and put my foot in it. I say, "This is what I think, and I don't care if you think it or not." Which is neither good tactics nor good sense in the structure of Parliament. But all this notwithstanding, I managed to get myself elected to represent Mid-Ulster in Westminster.

George Forrest, the Unionist Member for Mid-Ulster in the British Parliament, died on December 10, 1968. Later in the same month the Republican Party held a convention in Cookstown to select a candidate to contest the seat thus vacant. The Republican Party is illegal; so are Republican Clubs, and so are Republican conventions. Under the Special Powers Act, everybody in that hall could have been arrested and dumped into prison. But this was Northern Ireland. Everyone knew the convention was on; the delegates were falling out of the doors and windows; but there wasn't a policeman in the town who could have stopped it: "What Republican convention? Never heard of it!" I wanted to see what was happening, and went to the hall, but they wouldn't let me in and I came away again.

The main bone of contention among the Republicans was the policy of abstention: the Republicans used to stand on the basis that, if elected, they wouldn't go to Westminster and wouldn't take the oath to the British Queen. But this policy was going out of favor. Tom Mitchell had been the abstentionist Republican candidate at a few previous elections—he'd twice got elected in jail, where he was serving a ten years' sentence for an IRA arms raid on an army barracks; and, of course, as a convicted felon he was disqualified. But this time Tom refused to stand, except as an attendance candidate. The abstentionist tactic had been outplayed, he said: there was no longer any point in simply registering the number of Republicans at the polls. A lot of delegates followed Tom Mitchell's line, and the arguing went on for hours, from early in the evening until one o'clock next morning. I wanted to put my oar in and tell them it was better to stay a couple of hours longer than pick the wrong candidate. Which they did: they picked the wrong candidate. When stalemate between the abstentionists and the attendance faction was reached, one of the big guns of the party got up and said the official policy was still abstention and anyone who worked against it should get out. Rather than risk a split, everyone fell into line.

The candidate they picked was a solicitor, Kevin Agnew, a big, round, friendly man, a very ardent Republican of the old school, who would rather see the grass grow in the streets of his home town, Maghera, than surrender to the British. He was a reasonable enough choice for the abstentionist policy, but he couldn't convince those Republican voters who wanted a representative in Westminster that staying away was, in fact, still the best thing to do. With Kevin standing, the Republicans risked losing the seat disastrously. In the past voters hadn't minded if you went to Westminster or not, so long as you kept the Unionist out. But by now the civil-rights movement was having its effect, and people saw this by-election as an opportunity to project Northern Ireland into British politics and keep it there, even after the election was over.

Kevin wasn't, however, the only anti-Unionist candidate in the running. John Hume, one of the wealthier Catholics of Derry who had been much involved in the fight for social justice there and was to become one of the civil-rights leaders, was being considered as a civil-rights candidate. He might have been accepted by all the disunited forces of the opposition, but as far as the Republicans were concerned, Hume had blotted his copybook in the Stormont election by standing for (and winning) the Foyle constituency against the socialist program of Eamonn McCann. Austin Currie was also anxious to stand. Austin Currie is a shrewd, full-time politician who wants a seat in Westminster. His party, the Nationalist Party, is losing credit because people accept it has become the Catholic sectarian, "Green Tory," party, which is in no way progressive. In the February 1969 general election, when the Nationalists were generally going out of favor, Currie kept his seat in the Northern Ireland parliament by standing as a Nationalist with a mandate to form a new party. Thus he kept the declining Nationalist vote and won enough support from dissatisfied Nationalists to get back to Stormont. However, in the Mid-Ulster by-election, he had no prospect of getting to Westminster: the Republicans wouldn't vote for a Nationalist, and Currie couldn't hope to do more than split the vote, so letting the Unionist sail in. John Hume eventually dropped out of the bargaining, leaving Kevin Agnew and Austin Currie confronting each other, and everybody confronting the prospect of a Unionist victory. The whole thing was further complicated by a personal animosity between these two candidates: they would have stood down for Lucifer, but not for each other. Somebody would have to be forced between them.

In the middle of this situation, some of the Republicans came informally to me, observing in a casual way, "You could hold this seat." They came to me because I was becoming known as a speechmaker at civil-rights meetings, and as the Republicans told me, "You never *say* anything, but we know what you mean." It was a dishonest little game they were playing: they weren't prepared to allow a Republican to take the oath of allegiance, but they were prepared to go outside the party, find someone who believed what they professed to believe, and stuff that person up to Westminster to take the oath. So from Christmas to February 1969, hints were being dropped that Bernadette Devlin just might be the person to force a wedge between Agnew and Currie and hold the seat; but she was very young and she had no political affiliation.

It was not until I had fought the South Derry campaign that the Republicans began to view me seriously as a potential candidate who might be able to unite not only Republican and Nationalist voters, but Catholic and Protestant ones as well. Two delegates from the Republican Party came to my home in Cookstown early in March and put a proposition to me: if I would say I was standing, Kevin Agnew would withdraw and they would see that Austin Currie did too. But meanwhile lots of other people were clambering onto the election bandwagon, and all sorts of lunatics were claiming the right to represent the people in Westminster. Every day you looked at the newspaper, somebody else had announced he was standing. Saving the seat was becoming the major item in people's lives, and all sorts of drapers and cobblers and God knows who else were offering their names to solve the problem of selecting a candidate. *Everybody* in Mid-Ulster was prepared to stand. We faced the delightful prospect of there being so many candidates that everybody would lose their deposit and the seat would remain vacant. For on the Unionist side of the constituency as well, there were disagreements. The official candidate was Mrs. Anna Forrest, the widow of the MP who died. Mrs. Paisley and Mrs. Bunting couldn't settle which of their husbands should be allowed to stand, and the possibility was Paisley, Bunting, *and* Forrest. (This was an interesting little sidelight on Unionist history:

George Forrest had been the kind of Unionist who didn't hate Catholics—an ordinary, friendly sort of fellow who wasn't prepared to come out with the anti-popery stuff which Orangemen like to hear on the twelfth of July. A few years back, when Protestant extremism was growing, the Paisleyites stoned him off the twelfth of July platform, fired chairs at him, and kicked his head in. When the ambulance came to rush him to hospital, they blocked the road in the hope that George Forrest would die before he got there. But in the April 1969 by-election, a deal was done with the Paisleyites, and these same people turned round and voted for his wife.)

My immediate answer, when I was approached, was no; I didn't want to get caught up in parliamentary politics. I didn't want to give people a chance to say, "Look, the PD are political careerists like anybody else." And I thought it wouldn't do the civil-rights movement any good to get involved in a wrangle for a seat at Westminster. But more and more people kept coming to me, asking me to sort out the problem of too many candidates, and I thought the least I could do was see all the candidates and try and persuade them to decide among themselves who was the most suitable. Most of them would have nothing to do with me, so I went to the district's foremost political arranger, Mrs. McCluskey, and asked her if she knew of any way of getting all the candidates together.

She came up with the Unity Convention, a tactic she had already developed. It started as a brilliant idea, grew into the most farcical circus modern democracy has ever seen, and in the end produced a candidate. Mrs. McCluskey and her husband, Dr. Conn McCluskey, were working for social justice even before the civil-rights movement began. For years they collected facts and figures in Northern Ireland and fed them to Labour MP's in Britain, to the Council of Europe and the United Nations, to American congressmen, and to anybody else they could interest. They worked out the convention system as a means of organizing opposition to the Unionists, in the constituency of South Tyrone and Fermanagh at a previous Westminster election; and it almost succeeded except that at the last minute things broke down, the vote was split, and the Unionist Marquis of Hamilton took the seat.

For the Unity Convention, Mrs. McCluskey's first step was to write on a piece of paper a long list of all the anti-Unionists she thought were interested in the seat and of all the people who had been asked to stand. Then she put an announcement in the newspaper: "All these people, and anybody else interested in getting to Westminster, is invited to a series of public meetings." Potential candidates flocked to the first meeting: there must have been twenty of them, narrowed down to ten or so by the time they got to the platform. The names were all put into a hat and drawn out to determine the order of speaking, and each one had five minutes in which to put his case. I was there as someone who had been asked to stand, and it took me about two minutes flat to say my piece: "I am not a candidate in this election because I don't believe we will get the kind of unity I want—which is the unity of the working class, Catholic and Protestant. The unity being talked about here is Catholic unity. I think politics is basically a dirty job. I am not expert enough to play the dirty job clean, and I'm not prepared to play the dirty job dirty. My suggestion is that you should find from the rest of the platform the least dishonest person, and put him in."

Which didn't improve my reputation with the rest of the platform. I then left the platform and sat down in the body of the hall.

That first meeting was hilarious and disgusting and scandalous. The hall was packed with Catholics—who weren't there *as* Catholics, but as people anxious to oppose the Unionists—and in among all these Catholics a Protestant was discovered. He was Claud Wilton, from Derry, a member of the Liberal Party. Well, the hall went into raptures: "We're not sectarian! We have a Protestant in our midst!" And there was a standing ovation for "the Protestant who crossed the Great Divide." The firmness of my resolution not to stand began to waver when I found out how many people there wanted me in; and it took a steep dive downward when Austin Currie got up to speak. Austin Currie was standing, not as a Nationalist, but as a civil-rights candidate, and as such, he was preaching the most refined Catholic nationalism you ever heard. By the end of his speech, the audience had got it clear: "That's right—that's the sort of unity we want: all the papishes in together." After all the work the PD had done in the general election to break down religious bigotry and end the old vote-according-to-your-religion tradition, I couldn't bear to see Austin Currie go rampaging around and undo it in the name of our cause.

One of the people listed in Mrs. McCluskey's announcement in the newspaper was Michael Farrell, leader of the Young Socialists' Alliance and a formative influence in the Belfast PD. Half a dozen of us had a meeting in Michael's house to discuss whether he should stand, I should stand, or neither one of us should stand. Michael could have taken the Mid-Ulster seat: it would have been more difficult for him to create the right atmosphere than it was for me, and he might have won by a smaller majority. People identified with me for some reason—perhaps because I looked like their daughters or their granddaughters, or because I came from Mid-Ulster. I could stand up and say something and get a hopeful, emotional reaction; Michael could say exactly the same thing and the listeners interpreted it as fact, without any emotional drive behind it. But all the same, Michael was well-known in the area, having fought the general election in a neighboring constituency, and he could have won the seat, and have made much more use of it as a politician. He is quite simply much more politically mature and adept than I am. But he wouldn't stand—as a doctrinaire socialist, he wasn't prepared to get mixed up with the bourgeoisie and the fascists. No decision was made at that meeting about my standing or not: that was up to me, but while some of us argued that the by-election was pointless anyway and only gave people an unfounded hope that someone in Westminster could change things, other people thought it was important to keep Austin Currie out of Mid-Ulster. So I thought, and worried, and hesitated.

Then the people in South Derry who had voted for me in February got up a petition to ask me to change my mind and stand. The by-election wasn't only the concern of people in Mid-Ulster: everyone in Northern Ireland wanted the seat to be won. It wasn't so much me they cared about, or my policies, though after I was chosen they did to some extent listen to what I had to say, because it was different—neither the old sectarian nationalism, nor the old stay-away-from-Westminster Republicanism. However at this stage in the convention the thing that really obsessed people was getting one agreed candidate, and they would have voted for the floor mop to save the vote from being split. "All right," I said, "I'll run the whole circus to give the people who want to choose me an opportunity for doing so." But I still thought that when it came to polling day, I'd be back in the university and Austin and Kevin would fight it out together.

The next problem was that the Republicans, who had originally offered to withdraw their candidate if I would put myself up, decided that I had let them down by attending the Unity Convention. My attitude was that at least the convention gave people a chance to hear the lunatics who thought they should be in Parliament. They all meant well: I don't believe there was an opportunist among them; but they hadn't a clue about what was going on. One man, if elected, was going to chain himself to the railings of Westminster Hall, so that the MP's going in and out would be reminded of the Irish Question every day. He was so far advanced that he didn't know that MP's don't in fact sit in Westminster Hall. Another man's argument was that, as an IRA man, he'd been forced into ten years' exile in England by the Special Powers Act, and now hoped for a mandate to go back: most people thought that all he wanted was his fare to London. There was one man who at every meeting pulled out a pound note and said, "It's dirty British money!" To which everybody shouted back, "And you'll have about three thousand of them if you're elected." All these irrelevant issues, and in the middle of them, Kevin, Austin, and myself as the three main contenders.

Altogether there were about six meetings in the main towns of the constituency, and on paper it looked a very reasonable, democratic way of selecting a candidate. But in reality it didn't work that way. In Maghera, Kevin Agnew's home town and stronghold of the abstentionist Republican vote, the audience stamped their feet and rattled their chairs and shouted to drown the speeches; and in Nationalist areas, there was respectful silence for Austin Currie and heckling for everybody else. Because the Republicans were officially scorning the Unity Convention and all its works and pomps, Kevin Agnew didn't make speeches at meetings like the other prospective candidates; but he never failed to turn up, just to remind us all that he was in the running. I tried to persuade Mrs. McCluskey to put the weight of the convention behind Kevin's candidacy, for our tactics didn't seem to be working, and no one name was floating into general favor. But neither she nor anyone else would agree to back an abstentionist candidate. Mrs. McCluskey herself wanted Austin Currie to be chosen. Her husband was less interested. He is kind of eccentric, a very nice fellow: the idea of my getting elected amused him—what a dig in the ribs for society! What a kick in the teeth for politics! But he did want someone who would go to Westminster, and finally he just wanted the convention to be over, whomever we chose.

Selection day at last came. It was April 2, 1969, three days before candidates had to be nominated, and already one day too late to apply for postal votes. Each of the 135 electoral divisions in the constituency met to discuss the candidates and list them in the order of their choice; then they sent delegates, with instructions how to vote, to the central convention. The Republicans—the only shrewd party in existence in Northern Ireland—had steered clear of the Unity Convention, but they had no intention of seeing political initiative escape them. They went to the electoral division meetings, voted for Kevin Agnew, and got themselves elected as delegates to the convention. It was very noticeable, when the delegates trooped into the hall, that the majority of them just happened to be Republicans.

Names of the candidates were to be taken in alphabetical order. The first to be read out was Kevin Agnew. Everybody breathed a sigh of relief: if it had become clear he wasn't being considered, the Republicans would have walked out and the convention would have fallen flat on its face. Then the big moment of drama: when all the names had been read out, a man got up; he had a letter from Mr. Agnew which he wished to read. Permission was given. Mr. Agnew, in the interests of unity, was withdrawing from the election. And Kevin, in his absence, got a good cheer. Then Austin Currie, who was sitting near the back, got up: "I have an announcement to make." He sprinted up to the front of the hall. "In the light of Mr. Agnew's withdrawal, *I* also will withdraw." He did it with great dignity and definitely saved a lot of lost ground, but he knew the place was packed with Republicans who weren't in fifty million years going to vote for him, so rather than lose the nomination, he pulled out. That left me and all my mad friends who were going to chain themselves to the railings at Westminster and show the British. And I was elected.

I was hauled up to the platform, with people tripping over me and cheering and shouting, except one or two wiser souls who knew better than to cheer at a funeral. I made my little acceptance speech—we would beat the Unionists, and use Westminster properly, and work toward the day when we had no need to send people to Westminster.

Election day was fifteen days away. I had no deposit for my nomination; I had no nomination papers; I had no election machinery. We started organizing there and then, while the general meeting drifted out, dividing the constituency into areas and getting volunteers from among the convention delegates to start campaigning in them. We set up a committee: Loudon Seth was election agent, my Uncle Dan was treasurer, Eamonn McCann was press agent, and they and half a dozen others were the core of an organization that ran one of the most whirlwind campaigns in parliamentary history. We ended up on election day with almost as many workers as we had voters: we had lost the postal vote, because we were so busy selecting candidates that nobody thought of applying for it in time. So it was necessary to take the lame, the dying, and the dead out to vote. But by then we had enough cars to take everybody to the polling stations in style, whether they wanted to walk or not, and to ensure that some of the stations closed early because they had a 100 per cent vote in their area.

During the campaign we drew up a timetable of meetings. We started off with one meeting on the first night, two meetings on the second night, two meetings on most nights. Then we decided we could fit in three meetings a day. By the end of the campaign, we were running to five and six whistle-stop meetings a day; arriving at a housing estate, hopping out, holding a ten-minute meeting, then off again—just tearing frantically around the country. We covered every main town in the constituency, all the small towns, and even some of the smallest villages which had probably never seen a politician before. They were so far up the mountain, they weren't sure there was an election on. "Yes," we said, "there's an election, and this is the candidate." I was the goods to be sold, and my organizers were the salesmen.

Enthusiasm just snowballed until Election Day, April 17, when our slogan was: Never mind what Tories say. Today is D for Devlin Day!—as if we had already won the election. I was still sure we wouldn't, because I'd fought the election honestly on the nonsectarian, radical socialist policies I believed in. I was quite sure I'd alienate more Catholic Tory votes than I could make up for by an honest vote. Unfortunately the difference I made to traditional voting patterns was tiny. Mrs. Forrest didn't hold one public meeting throughout the campaign, but 29,000 people, mostly Protestants, gave her their vote. And too many Catholic Conservatives came out in support of what they saw as "the pan-papist candidate"; some of them were quite annoyed when the election results showed quite clearly that I had about 1,500 Protestant votes. One doctor said he thought it best not to read my political manifesto in case it put him off voting for me. So he didn't read it, he just threw it in the fire, and put his "X" behind the unity candidate.

So, by a majority of 4,211, Muggins got elected and dumped into Parliament.

Chapter 12

No sooner was the count complete than the press descended on me. To protect my brother and sisters from the attentions of the press, I was then staying at my aunt's home in the country, and on Friday, April 18, 1969, the day after polling day, reporters and photographers settled round the house like swarming bees, demanding idiotic, phony photographs of the MP sitting on a rug, surrounded by all her little cousins. They all took a fancy to the garden swing: everybody had to have photographs of "the swinging MP" —about the most obvious pun that any second-rate newspaper could be depended on to think up. The press were interested only in the gimmick publicity of the twenty-one-year-old female who makes it to be a Member of Parliament. Fair enough, I wasn't very professional in dealing with the press, but they weren't prepared to be helpful. As far as they were concerned, I was a mass of flesh which had become public property and they were entitled, at any hour of the day or night, to interrupt anything I was doing. They couldn't understand why I refused to allow them to take photographs of the MP getting out of bed in the morning; or the MP eating boiled eggs for breakfast. None of them wanted to ask the basic questions that would show why the situation in Northern Ireland should produce a "baby of Parliament."

That was the state of play on Friday. The next day violence flared again in Derry. I was going to Derry myself, and heard the reports of violence on the radio: it was common news at the time. A civil-rights march from Burntollet Bridge to Derry had been banned, and as a token protest some people sat down in the street in the center of the city. A few Paisleyites came out and the usual scuffles started. The police could easily have dealt with these disorders but their tactic, as ever, was to prevent clashes by beating the demonstrators off the streets. They charged the crowd, flourishing their batons, and the crowd fled in panic before them. Then somebody in the mass of people turned: this was how the real trouble started. "Why are we running from the police?" somebody said, and at that everybody stopped dead, turned round, and started beating the police back up the street. The police were armed with batons, shields, riot helmets, and, of course, their revolvers. The people had nothing, but they were angry enough to make up for the lack of weapons and they terrified the police who turned and ran. When the people saw the police fleeing for the first time in Derry, it was just too much for them, and they seized anything they could get their hands on and beat the police into the barracks. Then police reinforcements were brought into the city and the crowd, by this time trying to break into the barracks and slay all within, were driven off.

From then on, sporadic street fighting broke out in different parts of the city, and by the time I arrived at about ten o'clock in the evening, Derry was a battlefield. It was like coming into beleaguered Budapest: you had to negotiate the car round the piles of bricks and rubble and broken glass which were cluttering the roads. Every family in the Bogside, the Catholic slum ghetto of Derry, had left its home and was roaming the streets seeking whom it could devour. The police had arrived in their hundreds and pitched battles between the police and the Catholics were in progress. What had started as a clash between civil-rights supporters and Paisleyites had developed into sheer faction fighting between the Catholics and the police, and to the people of the Bogside, the police were fighting on behalf of the Protestants. Like soldiers coming back from the war, the police retired from the fighting to Fountain Street, the Protestant slum ghetto, for tea, sandwiches. and recuperation. When they could, the Catholics wanted to get up Fountain Street and beat hell out of the Protestants, who—for all that they had started it—were terrified. Mary Holland, *The Observer* reporter, and Eamonn McCann were in the Protestant area, trying to reassure people and promising that if an attack came, they would bring out the civil-rights movement in defense of the Protestants.

At this point we decided to give the Bogsiders something to do that would take their minds off wrecking Derry and slaughtering policemen. We got them to build barricades across the streets leading into the Bogside, so keeping them in their own area. (Ironically enough, in view of my part in this action, I was later summonsed to appear in court on four charges of inciting a mob to violence.) The barricades we built were very poor ones. They were built of planks and stones taken from a building site: a big mechanical digger on the site was found to be in working order, and we used it to lift loads of rubble, which were brought up to the barricades in this unwieldy contraption and dumped in the middle of the road. But the barricades, though high, had little base or substance, and in the end it took only one police truck to burst through them.

However the barricade-building was not just occupational therapy for enraged Bogsiders. We weren't in favor of attacking the police or spreading wanton violence through the streets, but we also felt the police had no business coming into the Bogside terrorizing people, and we wanted to muster our forces to prevent them coming again. For this reason we suggested that nobody should throw stones across the barricades at the skirmishing parties of police who occasionally burst round a corner, hurled a few missiles, then retreated again. Instead we advocated piling up the stones so we would have plenty of ammunition when it was needed. At first it was hard to get people to agree to this defensive policy: their argument was roughly that dead policemen couldn't come into the Bogside, anyway, but gradually tempers cooled and feelings dropped as the barricades went up.

Meanwhile the police were roaming round in totally undisciplined bands. A party of them went into one house, claiming to have seen someone run into it, and senselessly beat up everyone in the house. Others were going round saying, "If you see Bernadette Devlin, get her!" and "If you see Mary Holland, stone her to death!" For they don't like Mary Holland: she writes nasty things about them and takes it all down in shorthand when the police throw stones. But as the barricades neared completion, the police retreated, and people interpreted this as a certain amount of success. Coming up to midnight, there were only two more streets to barricade, and by this time nobody was any longer interested in going out to get anyone's blood. Some idiot had got up on the digger and was dangerously waltzing it in and out among the crowd, and people were good-naturedly dodging it and laughing, instead of getting on with the building.

Suddenly a boy yelled, "My God, they're coming!" Everybody stopped dead. It was one of the most horrific sights I have ever seen. High above us, the city wall was lined with a great silent mass of black figures. Slowly the mass started to move, down through the walls, into the two roads still not barricaded, and when the two battalions of police met, they joined forces and started a stomp toward us, beating their shields with their batons and howling dreadfully, in the manner of savages trying to intimidate their foes. Before this everybody just fled. Trapped in our own barricades, the nearest place we could flee to was a recently built high block of flats. Through megaphones we screamed to the people in the flats to open their doors to everyone but the police, and to the crowd not to panic but to walk as quickly and calmly as possible to safety. I took refuge, along with some pressmen, in one of the flats, and once we were in, the tenant put all his furniture against the door.

Then the police trucks came, dozens and dozens of them, smashing down the barricades, and wailing on through the Bogside like an invading army. There aren't many streetlights in the Bogside, but all the house lights were on and the lights in the High Flats. The roaming convoys of police vehicles traveled with headlights blazing, and the whole area was brightly and eerily lit when the police set fire to a builder's hut. The noise was terrible. Indoors everyone turned their radios on full blast, or played rebel songs at full volume on record-players, and people were singing the "Internationale" and "We Shall Overcome." Every time someone sneaked out of the High Flats to go home, the police made a dive at him, and tenants hurled down anything they had to let him make good his escape. But the will to hurt had gone: one bottle tossed from about the seventh story just missed a policeman's nose, and the woman who threw it shook for about fifteen minutes afterwards, she was so upset at the thought she might have killed him.

When eventually I left with my friends, the police didn't attempt to touch us, though we spat at them as we walked past. The next day, Sunday, with the police still occupying the Bogside, I left for Belfast. John Hume and Ivan Cooper, both civil-rights leaders in Derry, got the whole population of the Bogside to evacuate, took this crowd of several thousand people up Creggan Hill, and told the police they had two hours to get out. If they weren't clear of the Bogside by then, the people were coming back in, and the police would be responsible for the consequences. The police stuck it out until about fifteen minutes before the end of the ultimatum. Then they left.

That Sunday the wave of disorder spread to other parts of the country. A bomb explosion at the Silent Valley reservoir in the Mourne Mountains cut water supplies to Belfast and County Down; an electricity pylon near Armagh was sabotaged; and nine post offices, a bus station, and other buildings in Belfast were set on fire, some by petrol bombs. These acts of sabotage and violence were never pinned on anyone, but there were two very sophisticated schools of thought on who was responsible—at least for the attacks on water and electricity supplies. Where the two schools of thought differ is on which side of the Unionist movement they lay the blame. I thought for a time that these attacks were government-inspired. They were the sort of thing the IRA could be depended on to do, and I supposed that the government was trying to make a link in people's minds between the civil-rights campaign and the Irish Republican Army. It also gave the government an opportunity to call in the British Army without looking foolish. The odd thing was that the army was summoned to do guard duties, when the best part of the ten-thousand-strong force of reservist B Specials was still uncalled up and available. Could it be that the government didn't trust its own police reservists?

The other theory was that the Paisleyites had done the sabotage to intimidate not the civil-rights movement but the government. After his resignation, Captain O'Neill observed that dark and shadowy deeds had preceded all the important decisions made by his government over recent months; most likely these attacks were the work of extremists showing their strength and ensuring that the government reacted in a proper manner. But the attacks on post offices were undoubtedly done, on the personal initiative of someone or other, as a favor to the civil-rights movement. Post offices don't belong to the Northern Ireland authorities but to the Postmaster General in London, so an attack on them is one way to make your point in Westminster. Whoever was guilty, no one was ever caught, and the amnesty proposed in May by the new Prime Minister, Major Chichester-Clark, covered all these doings, and the activities of the police in Derry, and my four summonses as well.

That the British Parliament should hold an emergency debate on Northern Ireland five days after my election was not entirely the unprompted product of events. On Monday, April 21, the Home Secretary (Mr. Callaghan) announced in the House of Commons that he had agreed to make army units available for guard duties at essential installations in Northern Ireland. On the heels of this announcement Paul Rose, an English Labour MP who is chairman of the Campaign for Democracy in Ulster, successfully demanded the debate at which, it was planned, I would speak. The debate was fixed for the following afternoon, some twenty-four hours later.

Meanwhile, back in Belfast, aware that something was happening in Westminster but ignorant of the details, I was carrying out my first activity as a Member of Parliament. This was to sit in on a dispute between the Ministry of Agriculture, Toome Eel Fisheries, and a number of fishermen who were my constituents. From this I went on to dinner with the chairman of the fishermen's association and their solicitor, and it wasn't until nearly midnight that I managed to make contact with London. The instructions were terse: "Get over here." I was in Belfast; all my belongings were in Cookstown; and I didn't have any money. The rest of that night was spent traveling home to Cookstown, raising the cash for my fare, and getting back to Belfast in time to catch the first plane. Then the plane was delayed: there was supposedly a bomb on it. We all got off, and while the plane was searched, I fell asleep. On board again, I used the minutes before take-off to scribble a few points on the back of a telegram as the basis of my speech. At London Airport, hordes of photographers and pressmen were waiting: it was the sort of thing you see on the television news—some unfortunate creature and the press all huddling round. After the press conference, we came into London and stopped at the Irish Club in Eaton Square, where I was to stay. The members— and what a load of gombeen men they were—wanted to have a little victory celebration, but I couldn't wait for it. I had about two hours to have a bath, wash my hair, and find something clean to put on. The clothes I was wearing had been on demos, they weren't particularly clean, and they hadn't been off my back all night. But since I'd been whipped over to England so fast, I hadn't been able to get anything in Ireland and the obvious course was to go out and get it here. This, of course, was big news. Was I going down the Kings Road, center-of-the-with-it-fashion-industry? the press inquired. "Sure, anywhere," I said, so they all went down the Kings Road, and I went down Piccadilly with two women reporters. We bought clothes and a hairbrush and make-up, and set off in a taxi for Westminster, with me putting on make-up as we went. I tried to use the taxi mirror, but every time we turned a corner, I lost my face in it, and in the end one member of the press held my head steady, while the other put the make-up on, so that I didn't end with the foundation tube down my throat. This done, we pulled up at St. Stephen's Gate, and went into the House. There was no time to have first impressions, except that it was amusing to see policemen clearing the way instead of forming a cordon.

My sponsors, Paul Rose and Gerry Fitt, took me off for lunch in the Members' dining room. More stupid questions from the press: "Did you enjoy your lunch?" I said something to the effect that it was no worse than the Students' Union food, and this remark was evidently picked up by the catering manager. A few days later I received a little letter: they endeavored to provide a satisfactory service for all Members—particularly for those of delicate taste. That put me in my place. After that we went into the Whips' Office and had the wee rehearsal of bowing and pacing. You walk into the Chamber, up to the bar, and bow; five paces and you bow again; five more paces and another bow. You go forward to the Clerk, take the oath, and sign your name. Five paces and a bow to the Speaker. You shake hands with the Speaker. Then you go out the back door, all the way round, in another door, and sit down. So we went through this wee procedure, and it was great fun. When it came to the real thing, my sponsors had bigger legs and bigger feet than I had, and I took great big paces to make sure there were only five of them, not six or seven, and that we all arrived at the same spot at the same moment to bow in unison. The whole attitude of the House was, "Well, well, well! Look who's here!" Shaking hands with me, the Speaker said, "It is out of order for Members of the House to be jealous," and it was all very friendly and very frivolous: the Mother of Parliaments welcomes anybody in.

The Speaker was very helpful. He told me to wait for him when I went out the back door, then came out to say that I should simply stand up when I wanted to speak. So we went in, and the debate opened. Paul Rose was the first to speak, then Robin Chichester-Clark, the Westminster Member for Derry, got up with his "I was in the Bog-side . . ." I wonder how many times Robin Chichester-Clark was in the Bogside before he toured it by car the day after the riots. He went on to say that the civil-rights leaders, sincere as they were, had created a monster over which they had no longer any control and that the movement might have been respectable one day but we were now a lot of hoodlums and anarchists and Trotskyists and republicans.

I made my maiden speech after Chichester-Clark, and I didn't need my notes because everything I detested about the system was written in his Tory face. It was a bitter speech, but it wasn't in my own analysis of it a good speech. It merely stated that the situation was medieval, and that there was no longer anything to be gained from Westminster discussing it: the time for Westminster's discussion and Westminster's action had almost passed, and all they could do was decide which side of the House was going to take the blame for Northern Ireland.

The House thought it was delightful. Great stuff! Great sincerity! Which showed the House up for what it was. Somebody said something they really meant, without clothing it in nonoffensive language, without the formality of neatly typing it out and underlining the bits that were to be emphasized, and everyone said "Hear, hear!" The press was just the same. The press had built me up so much on the baby of Parliament, swinging MP, guess-whose-birthday-it-is-today angle that they couldn't in consideration of their own sales, turn round and condemn the speech. I made a scathing attack on Unionism and the whole British landlord invasion of Ireland, but even the Tory papers carried it. They'd got themselves into the position where they didn't expect me to make the kind of speech I made, and nobody, including me, thought I would have to make it so soon. Since then, since I've not been an exemplary Member of Parliament, the press in general have decided that I'm not the sort of well-mannered person the Victorians used to produce, and it would be better to say as little about me as possible. You know, she's got MP after her name, and she has no respect for it. She takes herself in among the workers and the unemployed and the squatters and the gypsies. A self-respecting Member of Parliament does nothing other than talk about these people in the House of Commons. They have discovered that their little child of Parliament is a monster who doesn't care about their Parliament, or their parliamentary system, or their parliamentary formalities, or their parliamentary parties.

When you look at the Labour benches and think, "Some of them must have got there honestly," you wonder what happened to them, and your constant watch is that it doesn't happen to you. Some of them warn you against becoming part of the system: the poor idiots that call themselves the Left warn you against the Right; but they are all tarred with the one brush—Parliament is what matters and the trouble about the workers on the factory floor is that they don't really understand. Not that you can expect them to understand: they're not MP's, they haven't gone through the Order Papers, they don't read *Hansard* daily to find out what somebody did in fact say in Parliament, they never get on any Select Committees. What could they know about running the country? Running the country is a game you play with the people on the other side of the House: a Tory MP stands up and asks the Secretary of State for Employment and Productivity (Mrs. Castle) what she intends to do about industrial relations, so that the Conservative Party can build its policy—could we please know your move on the board so we can work out our own strategy? And up jumps a Labour MP saying in effect, "If we build our structure properly, the Tories won't be able to build on top of it." Meanwhile the workers sit around wondering what's going on.

I find it impossible, outside the Chamber, to tell from what they say who is in the Labour Party and who is in the Tory Party. Sometimes there's an indication in the style of dress. There are about three styles of dress: the Tory in the smart tailored suit, running about the stuffy, dusty, dark, dank Houses of Parliament with a little buttonhole; the bourgeois Labour Party man who's got a good, well-cut, off-the-peg suit, and who is the real professional politician; and the big, ordinary workers' MP, with the coat hanging off him, who's against Harold Wilson on principle. Everybody's for and against things on the basis of who else is for or against them. The division bell rings, and people run in, scuttle out of every hole, even out of taxis: Gangway! the MP's coming! and in they all go, through the right door. How do they *know* the right door? How can they in conscience, having heard nothing of the debate, go and vote according to their party?

They really have forgotten what goes on outside. The only ordinary people they ever meet are by appointment in the Strangers' Bar. I have challenged one or two of them on forgetting where they came from, and they say, "Not at all! We have Labour Party meetings in our constituencies!" But most people who vote in an election aren't party members; they just live ordinary lives. They don't count. It's the people who come to meetings who are important, and you spend your whole life making excuses to them for the kind of policies you carry out. You brainwash them so that, at the next election, they'll go out and canvass for you. No matter what you believe in, you have to weigh it against the prospect of losing votes when the next election comes up; and better that you sacrifice your principles than you let a Tory in, for, as everybody knows, an unprincipled Labour man is better than a principled Tory. Half the time one feels that the Tories are more honest: at least they are open about their views on the place of the working class; but the Labour Party, whose attitude is exactly the same, cover it up with the claim, "We are the party of the workers." And none of them really has a clue what he's doing.

Nothing really matters! Parliament is just a friendly club. One man said to me, "We're all friends here—no politics outside the Chamber." This actually happened! And for me it summed up Westminster. One or two Members make a point of attending a workingman's club, but all the rest go to the same club and the same parties with the same friends. Their big word in conversation with me is "sincerity." We, the biggest phonies in the business, love sincerity. It's *so* refreshing! Makes us think of when we were young! How, by the way, are you settling down? Remember when I came into the House myself. Awfully difficult when you come in at a by-election. *I* came in at a by-election . . . And you feel like saying, "I wish to God you'd go out at a by-election." Some of them are indulgent about my running up the stairs and whistling in the corridors, but there's a general feeling that I ought to have more respect for the dignity of Parliament; ought not to be impatient with the pomp and ceremony and time wasted for "Hats off, strangers! Here comes the Speaker!" I always think of *Lord of the Flies* when they trot in with the Mace: "I've got the conch," there's no doubt about it.

You get more sense from the policeman at the door than from the Members of Parliament, and you learn more from him about how to work the system. The fellow on the door will tell you how to escape people, how Mr. Greenwood or Mr. Somebody Else avoids the people who come looking for them. He'll tell you, "I don't know why you bother to see people that come. Everybody else here ducks and hides. They all forget. Once they're in here, they all forget."

What I should do, according to the accepted view, is be a good child of Parliament, sit down and study the parliamentary methods, ask questions of the Prime Minister and be satisfied with the answers. I did have a try at asking Harold Wilson a question: he had said that the explosions in Northern Ireland made it impracticable to repeal the

Special Powers Act, and I put it to him that if common law couldn't deal with illegal explosions in Northern Ireland, he had better extend the Act to the rest of Britain and make sure that England, Scotland, and Wales were protected against possible explosions in the future. "I hope," says Harold, "the honorable Lady Member will discourage any such practices on this side of the Irish Sea." Then he toddled out of the House. Since he'd failed to answer my point, I got up to toddle after him and nail him in the corridor, but was stopped by my colleagues: "You can't treat the Prime Minister like that!" As far as I was concerned, old silver-haired, silver-tongued Harold was no better and no worse than I was, and his being Prime Minister was no excuse to waffle his way through the House of Commons, breaking promises as he went. In this sort of situation, there is not much I can do at Westminster for my constituents and Northern Ireland. All I can hope to achieve is to keep Northern Ireland's predicament as much before public attention as possible— and for that you get better results at workers' meetings than in the gentlemanly, all-friends-together club of the House of Commons.

The trouble in those early weeks was that I wasn't just an MP, however ineffective, but a phenomenon: I was the big international story. Which is a very time-taking and soul-destroying thing to be. If Michael Farrell had been elected, he would just have been an MP, getting on with the job within the limits of the possible, whereas I was not only failing to do anything for the people of Mid-Ulster; I was failing to do anything for God knows whom else as well. Masses of mail came in, most of it from other people's constituents, saying their own MP didn't care about them and would I take up their cause? They sent me their pension claims, and their wage claims, and their property problems, and their divorce cases, in the hope that I could sort it all out. They came in deputations to the House of Commons, and if they couldn't find their own Member, they sent for Berna-dette Devlin, their mediator with the gods: she can go where we can't, she can get round all the corners and find him for us. In theory it's easy enough to say their problems aren't my problems, but what do you do when you're face to face with someone in trouble? When, probably, you know perfectly well that the pig they're looking for is in the Strangers' Bar. You go trotting in and say, "There's a gentleman who seems very anxious to see you," and to woo him out into the open, you give the impression it's a rich donor, when all you've got is a wee cloth-capped paddy hoping to see his MP. The Members of Parliament don't like that: it's inter-fering in constituencies that aren't my business. I wrote to the Right Honorable Ian Macleod inviting him to a meeting for the gypsies. Back came his reply: "Thank you for invit-ing me to a meeting in my own constituency." This was sup-posed to snub me, make me feel: "Oh, I shouldn't have done that. That's the kind of thing that isn't done." Perhaps the strategy is to organize meetings in his constituency and *not* invite him.

As for the press, they weren't the slightest bit interested in the fact that I was (a) human, and (b) meant to be doing a job in London. In the end they went off me, but to begin with I had to change hotels every night, because the press kept finding out where I was. And not only were they inside the hotel when I got up in the morning, but they were all fighting over my bedroom door: I wakened to the din of squabbling photographers, and when I opened the door they all fell in. "Get out, you're getting no photographs!" I shouted. "Now, now, now," they soothed, "just five min-utes." But at the end of five minutes would they go away? Not on your life. Nobody wanted to be first to go in case something happened when he'd gone. So they all followed me into the street, milling around and knocking people down; and ordinary citizens got annoyed: they don't mind one way or another about Bernadette Devlin, but they are annoyed when a load of hoodlums with cameras walk all over them to take stupid exclusive pictures of her—"Berna-dette Devlin sucks an ice cream: the hot-head MP cools off."

Then Mary Holland and her husband took me in, but the press had no respect for these people who were kind enough to protect me from the world. Bit by bit they discovered the phone number and they would ring up at two, three, four in the morning, saying, "I wouldn't ring you, only it's urgent—is Miss Devlin expecting trouble in Ulster next weekend?" And I became the fortuneteller of Northern Ireland. A sort of harem of journalists, British and foreign, trotted round about two feet behind me. "I'll see you at four o'clock," I said. "I've already got appointments at one o'clock, two o'clock, and three o'clock. I'll see you at four." But they stayed with me, just to make sure. The chap I was supposed to see at one was already there at twelve, as were the chaps I was supposed to see at two, three, and four. So I come out, say I'm going to lunch, will be back as agreed at one p.m. All four decide to lunch with me, and all four try to get in my taxi. I tell them to pay for their own taxis, which they don't like. Then we all descend on some unfortunate man who runs a restaurant and all my attendant journalists want to sit at the next table and write down what I eat. They're not interested in politics: "We don't want the political article," they say, "everyone's done

the political article. We want the *real* Bernadette Devlin."
So they write down what I eat. If ever I was to get saying
something on Northern Ireland, I had to force it on them.
All they cared about was how, in these days of student riots,
does it feel to be a student in the Establishment? Or alterna-
tively, the girl from the bog makes good.

Then came the demands for television interviews, and I
spent my days scrambling from one television studio to another. "Why don't you say 'No'?" people asked. I *did* say no,
but it was a totally ineffective thing to say. The wee man
in the House of Commons that deals with telephone messages
was just on one constant run, up and down the stairs, with
messages from the same people. "Please ring Mr. Idiot,"
would come in at two thirty; "Please ring Mr. Idiot," would
come in at two forty-five. When I said no, it just meant this
particular demand went round to the back of the queue to
be put all over again.

Once I got a message in the House of Commons: "Caller
in United States to speak to Miss Devlin." I lifted the re-
ceiver and somebody down the other end of the line said
without further preamble, "You are now on our morning
show!"

"What the hell's your morning show, and who are you?"
I said. There were titters from the other end.

"That's a good answer from a frank person!" said my
unseen stranger, and I realized that half America was probably listening in. Another time I was asked to ring the international operator: a call from America had been booked and
paid for. Thinking it had to be important, if a call halfway
round the world had been paid for, I rang the operator, and
got routed through to Mrs. Typical Yank, who says, "Well!
Ah just wanted to get speaking to the real Bernadette Dev-

lin!" And that's all she wanted to say! Then she puts her family on to say "Hello!" It was the biggest circus in creation, as far as I could see.

The messages were many and varied, but above all they were many. "I'm sure you're busy, but would you please write us a five-thousand-word article?" Invitations poured in to tour America on the Irish circuit, the Irish-American circuit, the Negro civil-rights circuit, the university circuit —as though I was a traveling show. One invitation asked me to drop in on New Zealand and open an ecumenical meeting. Another one wanted me to pop over to Paris for half an hour and talk to a women's emancipation movement or something. Somebody else thought I could give a boost to international relations if I said a few words in a foreign language on Japanese television. And so the letters piled up, from Turkey, and Pakistan, and points east and west from Siberia to New South Wales—places which can't have the remotest interest in Northern Ireland and probably don't know where it is. One I rather liked came from Vietnam: its opening words were, "Hooray, hooray, hooray!"

Months after the by-election, I was still ploughing through a mountain of correspondence of some ten thousand letters and telegrams. Reactions to my sudden fame ranged from the Unionist Christopher Bland's view that I was Ireland's greatest national disaster since the famine; to the taxi driver's comment as he delivered me at the House one day: only two honest people had ever entered it—myself and Guy Fawkes. The Reverend Ian Paisley coined a nice phrase for me— "International Socialist Playgirl of the Year." I got several threatening letters, most of which were too melodramatic to be taken seriously: "Ten daggers are being sharpened for your back!" . . . or "You Fenian scum! You and all your

kind should be held under water till the bubbles come up!"
They dream up the most terrible deaths for you, which you
know are never going to happen because they are too ridiculous. Who is going to put ten daggers in your back when
one would do? One letter did frighten me. It was well written and it didn't have this note of hysteria. It said, "I hate
you. I hate Hume. I hate Cooper. All three of you will be
gunned down. Much as I hate you I don't want this to happen. But I have seen fifty new German revolvers and two
thousand rounds of ammunition. This is no joke. It is a
serious warning of danger. Signed, Loyal Protestant Supporter."

On the lighter side, I got proposals of marriage, mostly
from military men who, in consideration of their physical
fitness and stamina and so forth, believed they were master
races in themselves. With their beauty and my brains, they
suggested, we could get somewhere, and they sent references
to persuade me. For the cranky letters, I opened a special
file, and one which went straight into it read thus: "Dear
Madam, You are so beautifully evil that myself and my
fellow witches in the South Down coven have decided to
make you one of us." On such-and-such a night they would
invoke the Prince of Evil and, with the guts of a toad and
the legs of a cock and so forth, would initiate me into the
whole business. If ever I was to deviate from the path of
evil, the consequences would be disastrous. Two weeks later
the second "communication," as they called it, arrived to
say the initiation ceremony had gone off without a hitch,
the Prince of Evil had duly turned up, and would from now
on be ever at my side. "He will always be with you," I was
promised, "perhaps in the nod of a strange priest, or the wave
of an old man, the smile of a child, or the friendly brush of

a big black dog." This was wicked of them: of course people recognize me and nod or wave, and I'm supposed to think, "My God, I don't know that man! It must be the Prince of Evil." And every time a big black dog appears—of which there are millions—I'm meant to conclude that the Prince of Evil is keeping an eye on me. The letter ended, "This is the final communication you will receive from us unless you deviate from your work of evil." Whether I've deviated or not, I've so far heard nothing more on the subject.

Chapter 13

My function in life is not to be a politician in Parliament: it is to get something done. Though I didn't succeed in making it clear to my constituents, I soon satisfied myself that the whole grinding procedure of Parliament worked too slowly to be of any material use to the people of Mid-Ulster, and that Westminster, anyway, was basically indifferent to the problems of Northern Ireland. You can do a lot of talking, but nobody's listening, not in Westminster at any rate.

There is no doubt that the ordinary uncommitted people who voted for me at first felt I'd let them down. This was partly because of the anticlimax that followed the excitements of the election and the maiden speech. It is no ordinary by-election that gets 91.4 per cent of the electorate to the polling booths. In fact it was more of a mass movement than an election campaign: the voting was the smallest part, just the seal on two weeks of frantic enthusiasm and involvement. Then the maiden speech was made and rocketed all round the newspapers, and this added to the feeling that things were going to change. Most of my voters didn't know anything about politics—I don't know much myself, but I've learned quite a bit in a short time—and they couldn't understand why I didn't make another speech like that the next day. And I had no party machinery at home, through which to filter explanations to ground level.

The fact is that in the normal course of events Northern Ireland is hardly ever discussed in Westminster. Most of the points relevant to the Northern Ireland situation are the business of Stormont and are out of order in the House of Commons. Parliamentary questions have to be very carefully phrased to get through, and most of the time they bounce back at you with the message: Refer to the appropriate department in Stormont. Only the Post Office, which is the business of the Postmaster General in London, and the security of the nation are proper subjects for Westminster, so, apart from the siting of a new telephone kiosk or the warding off of a foreign invasion, what can you achieve? In order to get five minutes on Northern Ireland, you have to go through a long process of wooing, compromising, and twisting, and as far as I'm concerned, the effort isn't worth the result, on which nobody is going to act anyway. A Member of Parliament representing an English constituency can probably, if he's prepared to, use the system to the benefit of his constituents; but the Northern Ireland MP is hardly more than a public relations officer, getting paid £3,250 a year for a nonexistent job. The big problems in Mid-Ulster are industrial unemployment—most people who have work are obliged to travel outside the constituency to get it; agricultural inefficiency—the uncompetitive small farmer is unashamedly being forced out; and the fact that the fishing industry of Lough Neagh is controlled by four individuals who don't even belong to Northern Ireland. And there is simply nothing I can do about these problems. as a Member of Parliament in Westminster.

What I *can* do is get a post box for Slate Quarry. Slate Quarry is a small dying village, the least of whose worries but the only one I can help with, is the absence of a post box. If you work it out, the biggest economic scandal in Britain is that someone can earn £3,250 a year for getting three fishing licences, one clear-way to a garage, and a couple of telephone kiosks.

Long after this miserable situation was clear to me, the attitude of many of my constituents was still, "You're a great wee girl! You're doing a grand job!" They didn't have a clue what I was doing, but my picture got in the papers and they were certain a grand job was being done somewhere. Lots of people in Cookstown just wished I'd come home oftener, not to discuss things with them and solve problems, but to be on view, to shake their hands and pat their children on the head. Perhaps eight thousand of my thirty three and a half thousand votes were honest, political votes, in that the electors—mostly Republicans and a few Protestant socialists—believed in the policies I preached. But for the rest, though I fought my campaign honestly, very few of them saw me as meaning every word I said: that I didn't want to be a politician; that I didn't think one person at Westminster could change things; that I believed socialism was the way to get justice. These people of the majority want a miracle, the whole Ulster situation transformed almost overnight; and I can't do the miracle. In fact, it was the wrong tactic to let people think that getting an MP into Westminster was helping the civil-rights cause. What I should have done was stick my neck out, attack segregated education, the

Orange Order and all the other sacred cows of the ruling Tories, and lose the election.

Several thousand of my votes were definitely dishonest. They came from Nationalist sympathizers who told themselves, "We don't agree with one solitary word she says, but better a Catholic we don't agree with than a Unionist." Interestingly enough, this vote-according-to-creed pattern broke down a bit in my own home town, where my Unionist opponent, Mrs. Forrest, also lived. There were people in Cookstown who, despite the fact they shared my religion and had always voted on religious lines before, said they wouldn't vote for me: I came from the wrong end of town. This was promising, but it didn't go far enough, and there was a large bloc of middle-class Catholic electors who put me into Parliament in the hope they could control me afterwards. They saw me as the Catholic MP who would organize Mid-Ulster for the Catholic middle class and give them Catholic power. What they wanted was a big drive to get all the Catholics on the electoral register: I was only prepared to work on the registers for all the population, Catholic and Protestant alike. So when I refused to take part in their little schemes, I was called to book at the "Maghera Parliament." Captain O'Neill had his "Portadown Parliament," where the plot to overthrow him was first concocted: I had my Maghera Parliament.

This was a group of young people who gave themselves the job of advising me. Some of them only meant well, some hoped to manipulate me. The Maghera Parliament, which met several times and had a final explosive meeting with me midway through May, had two main grievances. The first was that I was being taken over by the Reds. They wanted to hear no more of this socialism: socialism was communism; communism was anti-Catholicism; it was time I got down to work on the lines mapped out by them. The second grievance was my friendship with Loudon Seth. All right, he'd been a good election agent, they agreed, but he was an agent for something else as well, either Communist or Unionist, I could take my pick. Their real objection was that Loudon was a Protestant in the process of being divorced by his wife, and they didn't like their respectable middle-class Catholic reputations tarnished by such associations. At one stage they promised to produce for me within twenty-four hours undeniable evidence that he was a Communist agent. "Fair enough," I said. "Produce it. And I will personally kill him myself." But the next day the evidence was not produced.

"How about the Communist-agent evidence?" I said.

"We'll get it! We have it!" Still it failed to come. If they'd had the wit, they would have manufactured it; as it was, the ploy was a failure. But they had other objections: I would have to behave myself, I was told, in a respectable fashion befitting a young Irish Catholic girl representing her country in England. There was to be less of this smoking in public. There was to be no drinking: it gave a bad image of the Irish people. You would have thought I was a drunkard, the way they were going on. And there was to be no more fraternizing with common workers in England, getting mixed up with May Day processions and the like. We were back to my supposed Communist allegiance. I lost my temper at that meeting and told them to find another Christ to crucify, for this one was humping down off the cross; at which they all came groveling out saying, "You're overtired, take a holiday." They planned to write a letter to the newspaper, listing my faults to the constituency. "Go ahead," I said. "Write whatever you like. But write it carefully, because if you make one false statement, I'll sue you for defamation of character." They didn't choose to take the risk.

The Maghera Parliament weren't the only plotters I had to deal with. No sooner was I elected than there were so many daggers in my back I could hardly keep on my feet. There were two main grounds for resentment: as the girl-MP I was mopping up everybody else's publicity, and the envious said, "Before she gets any bigger, we'll take the ground from under her." And, secondly, I was seen as a threat to the United Opposition. The United Opposition was an attempt by the fragmented Opposition in Stormont to pit its combined strength against the Unionists. Ever since the February 1969 general election, people had been demanding a united front between these MP's, whose beliefs stretched from Catholic Toryism to Catholic Democratic Socialism, having only Catholicism in common. Apart from internal dissensions on beliefs, the thing that prevented the united front from coalescing was the problem of who should lead it. There were three contenders for leadership—Austin Currie, John Hume, and Gerry Fitt, and no one of them would accept either of the other two. So when I was elected to Westminster, there was a tendency to say, "Why doesn't Bernadette Devlin lead the United Opposition?" I wasn't prepared to lead any Catholic alliance, but the would-be leaders feared me all the same, and planned to discredit me by publicly dissociating themselves from "irresponsible statements" I'd made about the good Prime Minister of Britain. The best friend I had in Stormont was Ivan Cooper: not only did he keep me informed of the progress of the plot, but he told them he was having nothing to do with their discrediting operations, and that plot also fizzled out.

But the plotters in the end will win. In the end it will be people who voted for me who will stand in my way, prevent me from working for my beliefs, and generally sling me out on my neck. Which is sad. I didn't set out to fool anybody by presenting myself as other than I am, but everyone has invented their own little imaginary Bernadette Devlins. They called me St. Joan of Arc, and St. Bernadette, and the second Messiah, and God knows what other heresies they didn't think of. When I turn out to be different from the image they have of me, they don't say, "I formed a wrong impression of that girl"; they are just broken-hearted that I have "let them down." I have to live with this.

I think my life will always be worth living, though I don't imagine it being very easy. I can't, for instance, see myself having much personal privacy, or being simply Bernadette Devlin ever again. Even when I'm no longer a Member of Parliament, when I go back to being a student, I'm still going to be that Bernadette Devlin who used to be an MP, and everywhere I go, I'll drag with me the memory of my face plastered across the newspapers. I can definitely rule out a future as a parliamentarian, but I don't suppose I shall ever escape from political involvement, if for no better reason than my sheer inability to mind my own business. In reality, I'm an ordinary person who wishes the situation in Northern Ireland and elsewhere were such as to allow me to go about my own interests, which are essentially academic. I wish I could just concentrate on being a good psychologist. But if you're aware of what's going on around you, and get caught up in problems which are so blatant, you can't just worry about your own concerns. So I expect always to be involved in action. As a Member of Parliament, however, I can only see I have a choice of ways to lose: either by doing nothing, accepting the system, becoming part of the Establishment, and losing whatever is left of my integrity; or by keeping my integrity and losing my public, for whom I haven't done miracles, freed the people, produced civil rights, or lived up to the image of St. Bernadette.

Basically I believe that the parliamentary system of democracy has broken down. What we have now is a kind of *Animal Farm*, all-pigs-are-equal system, whereby the pigs with MP after their name are entitled to sit in the farmhouse, and the rest of us are just common four-footed animals. At one moment you are an ordinary person fighting for the rights of the people, and then you become an MP, and your place is in the Establishment, in the Chamber making wise statements, in the Strangers' Bar telling the people who told *you* what they want, what in fact they want; and telling them not only did they want it, but they're bloody well getting it. Anywhere the parliamentary system is in force, you find the same inherent defects: the representatives, once inside the structure, no longer represent. Which, maybe, has already happened in Mid-Ulster. But the advocates of parliamentary democracy win out against people like me when it comes to saying what to put in its place. Obviously there has to be some kind of structure: you can't have mass democracy on the level of running a country; but something is wrong with a structure which represents so few of us; and it *is* unrepresentative, otherwise there wouldn't be such conflict and outcry every time Parliament does something.

Even if it were reformed, Parliament is all too slow and abstract for someone like me. What I want is action, involvement. The sort of political development I want to take part in is the growth of militancy from consistent positive action against the Establishment. I would like to see mass squatting campaigns—not only in Ireland, for Ireland doesn't have a monopoly of the housing problem. This has already begun in Derry. In Derry last summer the Derry Labour Party found out who was getting new houses, then went round to these people and asked them to say when they were moving out of their old home, so that the squatters could move somebody in. Only a few outgoing tenants were not prepared to help. In some cases they were vacating their homes because the house was condemned, but often the old house was due to lie empty for years, waiting for some grand development scheme to catch up with the area, and meanwhile deliberately kept vacant by the local authority. In all cases, the houses were better than the lodgings the squatters came from. But the local council, to prevent illegal tenants coming in, would send round a man with a sledge hammer to rip up the floorboards and take out the staircase. That was why it was important to know when the outgoing tenants planned to move.

Then the council got wise to this, and the man with the sledge hammer arrived on moving day. "Have you finished with the lavatory, ma'am?" he'd say. "Yes, we won't be needing it again." Smash! "Are you planning to light the fire today?" "No we're going shortly." Crash! And so, as one by one the rooms were emptied, they were reduced to unlivable-in shells. The squatters thought up a new tactic: they moved a family into the house to spend the last day with the people who were leaving, so for twenty-four hours the house held double families and double furniture.

This sort of activity shows people, Catholic, Protestant, or unaffiliated, the clash of interests between the people and the powers that be. It shows them that those condemned as troublemakers are actually doing something positive to help, whereas the local authority is reacting by wrecking and evicting and generally making people's lives miserable. In the first six months of 1969, the Derry Labour Party, under the active leadership of Eamonn McCann, housed more families than all the respectable housing bodies in Derry put together. In such ways sympathy is built up, and turns eventually into material support.

I saw it happen in Ilford, near London, where the local council employed a private army of bailiffs to get squatters out of broken-down property, which the Ilford squatters had spent days and their own money on making not only habitable but attractive. I went down to Ilford when the eviction attempt was happening, in June 1969, and I would have liked to say, "To hell with Parliament," and helped the squatters dig their trenches and put up their barbed-wire barricades. All I did do was give some money for the buying of more barbed wire: probably parliamentary salary has never been better spent. Then I went back to Westminster, planning to get some of the Liberal MP's, like Jeremy Thorpe and Eric Lubbock, to organize some sort of protest about the council's strong-arm methods. But I couldn't find anybody, and if I had, nothing would have happened: people would have stood up in the House of Commons and said, "Private armies are disgusting, they're utterly condemned, yes!" And they would have sat down again, and nobody in Ilford would have noticed they'd opened their mouths.

Despairing of Parliament, I returned to Ilford on the principle that if it came to throwing stones, I'd be one more to help. It didn't come to that, but what *was* happening was that respectable citizens like doctors were coming round to the squatters with food and odd bits of furniture to replace the furniture that had been wrecked. They were *involved;* they'd done something even if it was no more than bring a quarter of tea into an illegal tenant's home.

Someone more patient than me, someone who could put up with Parliament's lack of involvement with real people, would have worked at the legislation angle. If Michael Farrell, instead of Bernadette Devlin, had been elected for Mid-Ulster, he would have got his supporters and put up his private bill and outlawed the use of such methods. But even Michael Farrell couldn't make it work for Ulster; we're very fond of our private armies in the North of Ireland, and only if Stormont chooses does the law of the rest of Britain get passed on to us. Theoretically I might do a brilliant job of cleaning up the position of the underprivileged in England; and leave the people of Mid-Ulster precisely where they are.

But basically I'm against the British Parliament anyway: what right have they to sit there lording it over us? Perhaps the Reverend Ian was right, and I perjured myself by taking an oath of allegiance to the British Queen. At the time the maiden speech seemed important. But what I would have liked to do was swear my allegiance to the common people, and have a socialist government throw me out for doing so.

Chapter 14

Both inside and outside Parliament I'd lost a great deal of popularity by the time my first session at Westminster ended in the summer of 1969. To begin with, I was the greatest publicity gimmick since Kraft cheese slices, but it wasn't long before people discovered the final horrors of letting an urchin into Parliament. The British had shown what grand democrats they were: anybody—even a Northern Ireland brat of twenty-two—was allowed to sit in their House of Commons. And what did these ungrateful Irish peasants do, when you made them Members of Parliament and gave them £3,250 a year? They simply went off home and threw stones at you.

But I decided other people's attitudes didn't really matter and I left London to settle down to work in the constituency. I'd a number of things on my program. I wanted to go to America to collect money for the civil-rights movement. More particularly I wanted to campaign for funds to start self-help schemes in the constituency, especially among the farmers. I was also going to do a lot of hard study and turn up in Parliament in October having read all their books and beat them at the parliamentary game as well.

Such were my intentions. Events were to prove that I might as well not have bothered to plan.

Ever since Major Chichester-Clark's election as Prime Minister, a sort of false calm had prevailed in Northern Ireland, but below the surface the whole situation was becoming more and more tense. The twelfth of July, the great Protestant celebration of King Billy's victory over James II and his Fenian hordes, was a curtain-raiser for the violence to come. In Derry the tension exploded in riots during which the Bogside took most of its own area apart. It was the first occasion on which there was massive looting in Derry, and all the respectable leaders of the community condemned it, failing to realize that the "hooligans" were quite simply frustrated people wrecking everything because they couldn't find any other way of expressing their discontent. Once again the trouble in Derry spread across the country. In Dungiven—a town that is almost 90 per cent Roman Catholic —the Catholics burned the Orange Hall to the ground and tried to take the burnt stone apart with their hands. But there was no immediate sequel: tempers were calmed on the surface, the hooligans were put back in their cages and their ghettos, and the country settled down to wait in some suspense for August 12.

August 12 is the day of the Apprentice Boys' Procession in Londonderry, which celebrates the defense of the besieged city by the apprentices in 1689. These young boys, against the orders of their betters and wisers, closed the city gates and encouraged the population to fight off the besiegers, many of them dying at their posts, until the relief ships reached Derry one hundred and five days later. So every year a procession some twenty to thirty thousand strong processes round the walls of Derry to ensure they've not been breached since last year, and normally no one pays any attention to it—it's just part of Northern Ireland's pageantry, one which, ironically enough, celebrates a struggle for civil and religious liberty. But by August 1969, the procession could be seen only as a provocative political act, and leaders of many sections of the community, Protestant and Catholic, asked the government to put a blanket ban on marching until feelings cooled and reforms could be brought in which would create better relations between the townspeople in any given area. But the government, which by this time had totally abdicated its responsibility to govern, refused to stop the procession on the grounds that it was traditional, and the pomp and ceremony for August 12 continued.

It led to further disorders. An Orangemen's parade in Belfast stopped outside a Catholic block of flats and dosed the Papishes with "God save the Queen" and a volley of stones. In return a bottle was hurled at the bandleader, and the resulting scuffle quickly escalated into general wrecking and rioting, but with a new twist: the people in the Protestant slum area began looting and ravaging their own district, just as the Catholics had done in Bogside, and from equally irrational motives. They felt their whole heritage was being threatened and the government whose power base they were was doing nothing for them, so in the traditional pattern, they vented their frustration on their own property. Completely failing to understand all this, the Unionists turned round and called their own supporters hooligans. It was a great blow to the Protestant working class: after all they had done for the Unionists, in return for the little the Unionists had done for them, they were being classed as antisocial elements. Their allegiance began to slip. Knowing they were losing contact with their grass roots, Major Chichester-Clark and his ministers didn't dare to ban the Apprentice Boys' Procession. It would have seemed the final sell-out. So it went ahead.

Remembering what the police action had been on every other public occasion in Derry over the past twelve months, the people of the Bogside decided that, for their own safety, they would ignore the procession, mind their own business, and stay in the Catholic area outside the city walls with their heads down until it was all over. But if the twenty thousand marchers came down to attack them, after a day's celebration and drinking, they would defend their homes. The Bog-siders' gesture toward peace was met with provocation. From the walls overlooking the Catholic slum, the marchers and their supporters hurled taunts about keeping Catholics shut up in rabbit hutches. "All Fenians ought to be penned in, anyway," they yelled. Finally the attempts to goad the Catholics out succeeded in a small way and a few squabbles broke out between the marchers and the Bogsiders. Rather than sort the squabblers out and send them on their separate ways, the police decided a baton-charge was in order and made a run into the Bogside. Promptly the barricades went up, but this time the police decided they were not going to tolerate the Bogside's resistance to being beaten into the ground. "We've got to beat them this time, Miss, or we're done for," they told Mary Holland of *The Observer*.

And so the Battle of the Bogside began. It was then about four o'clock in the afternoon of August 12. Not for another fifty hours did the day-and-night fighting stop, and when it was over, it was the police who retreated. The Bogside was still unbreached, and the Unionist government was a great stride nearer its downfall.

The Battle of the Bogside, according to Major Chichester-

Clark, was part of a planned conspiracy to overthrow the government. If the Major had seen inside the barricades he would have found something much stronger and more terrifying than the plots of any organization. What was happening there was that ordinary, peaceful people, who had no desire to spend fifty hours throwing stones and petrol bombs, had realized the harm that had been done to them for half a century and were learning how to fight in self-defense. We threw up barricades of rubble, pipe, and paving stones—anything we could get our hands on—to prevent the police coming straight into the area and, in their own words, "settling the Bogside once and for all." Within the first half hour, eight police tenders were trapped in our barricades, and if only we'd had the means to destroy them we would have burned those tenders out.

It was at that point that the manufacture of petrol bombs began. The petrol bombs were made, literally, by pregnant women and children. Kids of seven and eight who couldn't fight made the petrol bombs, and they made them pretty well. The kids of nine and ten carried them in crates to the front lines. The young girls collected stones and built the barricades, and the girls, the boys and the men fought on the front line against the police. The police answered our stones and petrol bombs with stones of their own, and with ever-increasing supplies of tear gas. The whole air was saturated with it, and we had not a gas mask among us. I telephoned the Southern Ireland Minister of Defense to beg him to send us a thousand gas masks for the children at least. I was willing to claim I had stolen them, I said, if he didn't want us to have them openly. But he wouldn't cooperate. Jack Lynch, the Premier, was making grand-sounding statements from Dublin about his readiness to march to our defense. But he was only playing politics: such a march would have been tantamount to a declaration of war on England, and Mr. Lynch is economically tied to Mother England's apron strings and his army is no match for the British. In any case, in the middle of the twentieth century no two Western European powers, however unimportant, are going to declare war because everybody is frightened of what the Russians would do when their backs were turned. We got medical supplies from the South, but gas masks we had to go without. So we made do with wet blankets, with cotton wool steeped in vinegar, with handkerchiefs soaked in sodium bicarbonate, and we fought on through the night, all through the next day and the following night and into the third day, and we showed the police that nothing they did was going to beat us.

Meanwhile what was left of my reputation was taking a beating in the newspapers. All the papers were carrying photographs of Bernadette Devlin, bejeaned, besweatered, and besieged in the Bogside, leading people on and organizing the manufacture of petrol bombs and hollering at the people through megaphones to "throw them hard and throw them straight"; or organizing little guerrilla troops of a hundred men, in ten rows of ten men, to run like hell down side streets and catch the police in the middle, making sure that everybody had two petrol bombs and somebody got a copper. But what the press said about me didn't have the effect they intended. I didn't have time to read the papers myself—I was always on the barricades; and other people in Northern Ireland, who had begun to take the discrediting line fed them by the British press, could see that what I was doing was necessary. "If they come in here to get Bernadette Devlin, we'll slaughter them all," they said.

While we fought on, the Civil Rights Association organized demonstrations in ten other towns, hoping this would take police pressure off Derry and allow us a certain amount of relaxation in the struggle. These demonstrations were held in defiance of the government's ban, imposed as soon as the Apprentice Boys had stopped marching, but they failed in their object. Instead of withdrawing policemen from Derry, the government called out the B Specials. Three hours later Harold Wilson sent the British Army into Derry, and the B Specials were switched to Belfast to wreak havoc on the citizens. There are no regulation tests to get into the B Specials. You don't have to do an eye test; you don't have to have a minimum or a maximum height; there are no weight restrictions and no intelligence qualifications. All you've got to be is a supporter of the government, but once you're in you are entitled to service pay, to a gun, to all the ammunition you want, and to a uniform which is usually either two sizes too big or three sizes too small.

In Belfast the B Specials, alongside the police, fought the demonstrators. They did more. With small arms, machine guns and armored cars, they launched a vicious, well-planned attack on Catholic areas. They burned down row upon row of houses. Only the arrival of the British Army brought their destructive progress to a halt, and I have no doubt myself that the army came, not because Major Chichester-Clark asked for help, but because Harold Wilson wasn't prepared to tolerate the Unionist Party's private army of reserve police. The soldiers got an ironic reception: while the Unionists, who have always been the Union Jack wavers, stayed cool, Republicans and Nationalists cheered the arrival of British troops on Irish soil.

But the barricades stayed up. The fighting was over, for

the moment at any rate, but our demands had still to be met. One of these was an amnesty for every civilian in Northern Ireland, Catholic or Protestant, who had been forced into illegality. We leafleted the Free State Army, asking them to desert and come to our aid. We campaigned among the British troops, asking them to do the same thing. I believe they call it sedition. There was some doubt whether I personally was guilty of treason or not. I'd thrown stones at policemen (unfortunately I can't throw straight, and they missed). According to Major Chichester-Clark, I'd incited Bogsiders to rebellion and plotted the overthrow of the state. But the situation in Northern Ireland was such that nobody cared. It was the government who interned, without trial, people whose only crime was their political viewpoint. It was their men who set up kangaroo courts, murdered children, burned families out. Our sin was the lesser, and we will win in the long term, or the short.

Derry suddenly found itself the center of revolutionary Europe, setting a pattern that revolutionaries the world over will never forget. It was very interesting to note that in Czechoslovakia in August 1969 they followed our pattern, perhaps unconsciously. As soon as the troops came in, the people raced down side streets and put up barricades. Demonstrators in Dublin did exactly the same thing when they protested at the British Embassy. And they did it in London. It became the fashion to throw up barricades between yourself and the forces of the law and pelt them with petrol bombs from the other side. We had an influx of foreign revolutionary journalists searching for illumination on the Theory of Petrol Bomb Fighting. The people of the Bogside thought it was fantastic: they didn't know how to spell revolution, never mind work it out, but they were really delighted with themselves that people should come from the Sorbonne to ask the unemployed of Bogside where they learned to fight so well.

But behind the farcical aspects of the whole affair lay a serious problem: these people, out of fear, could never go back to the situation before August 12, 1969. We reached then a turning point in Irish history, and we reached it because of the determination of one group of people in a Catholic slum area in Derry. In fifty hours we brought a government to its knees, and we gave back to a down-trodden people their pride and the strength of their convictions.

It is very difficult to forecast what will happen next. For fifty years things have been static in Northern Ireland, and we are catching up on fifty years' history in the period of a year. Every day means a new chapter in a book and a new chapter in the life of a person. But whatever happens, never again will the Unionist government be able to govern Northern Ireland as it has done since the country was created by Act of Parliament. The people have made their situation clear. We will fight for justice. We will try to achieve it by peaceful means. But if it becomes necessary we will simply make it impossible for any unjust government to govern us. We will refuse to have anything to do with it. We will build our own houses and refuse to pay rent on those houses to the government. We will take control of our own areas and we will run them. We'll build our own factories, we'll pay taxes to our own people, and the government can sit in Stormont and govern whoever will put up with it, for more and more people will stand by a fair system, however illegal, than will stand by a discredited government. The Unionists can struggle as much as they like to get back the support of the Protestant working class, but we shall get through to the Protestants in the end. Some of them have burned down Catholic homes, but we will not allow our forces to terrorize the ordinary Protestant population. One day they will realize we have no more quarrel with people who happen to be Protestant than with people who happen to be Catholic. They will see that our only quarrel is with the Unionist Party government.

For half a century it has misgoverned us, but it is on the way out. Now we are witnessing its dying convulsions. And with traditional Irish mercy, when we've got it down we will kick it into the ground.

VINTAGE CRITICISM,
LITERATURE, MUSIC, AND ART

A free catalogue of VINTAGE BOOKS *will be sent at your request. Write to* Vintage Books, 457 Madison Avenue, New York, New York 10022.